SUCCESS AT MEDIATION

SUCCESS AT MEDIATION

How to Define and Accomplish It

Practical Observations and Recommendations

RAYMOND G. CHADWICK JD

Chadwick Mediation & Arbitration, LLC
(706) 373-9383
www.chadwickmediation.com
rchadwick@chadwickmediation.com

This book may be ordered by contacting:

Raymond G. Chadwick JD
2714 Hillcrest Avenue
Augusta, Georgia 30909
rchadwick@chadwickmediation.com
(706) 373-9383

ISBN: 1516841166
ISBN 13: 9781516841165
Library of Congress Control Number: 2015913046
CreateSpace Independent Publishing Platform
North Charleston, South Carolina

I want to give a very special thanks to my good friend Gerald T. Chambers, Ph.D., my volunteer editor who spent many hours reviewing, correcting and improving my initial drafts of this book. He made me uncomfortably aware of all I have forgotten since 10th grade English class – rules of grammar, proper sentence structure, punctuation, tense and expressing clarity of thought. I am glad I am not one of his students graded on my drafts.

TABLE OF CONTENTS

ABOUT THE AUTHOR

Ray Chadwick, a graduate of the University of Virginia School of Law, was a partner in the Litigation Practice Group of his law firm until his retirement. During his 32 years of active litigation practice, he represented plaintiffs and defendants in a wide variety of legal matters and tried cases involving medical malpractice, products liability, breach of contract, business disputes, construction defects, employment discrimination, wrongful death and personal injury. He began representing clients in mediations in 1989 and, following retirement from his firm, became a full time mediator and arbitrator. He has also been appointed to serve as a special master for cases in state and federal courts.

Ray is a registered mediator and arbitrator with the Georgia Office of Dispute Resolution and has served as Chair and member of the Executive Committee of the Dispute Resolution Section of the State Bar of Georgia. He has been appointed by the Supreme Court of Georgia to serve on the Georgia Commission on Dispute Resolution and to chair its Liaison Committee for registered neutrals in Georgia. Ray has chaired and made presentations at numerous programs on mediation for the Georgia Institute of Continuing Legal Education and other programs for both practicing attorneys and mediators. He has been named in The Best Lawyers in America® for mediation and arbitration since beginning his full time practice in those areas. Ray is the principal of Chadwick Mediation and Arbitration, LLC.

INTRODUCTION

This book presents what I have learned, or think I have learned, about litigation and mediation. It is principally based on:

* Preparing, trying or settling cases the "old fashioned" way, direct lawyer to lawyer negotiation for over 30 years;
* Representing clients in mediations for over 20 years;
* Completing the extensive training required to become a registered mediator and arbitrator in Georgia;
* Serving as a mediator, arbitrator and special master;
* Chairing, making presentations, and listening to others make presentations on mediation, arbitration, early neutral evaluation, and special masters at numerous continuing legal education programs; and,
* Discussing mediations and exploring mediation techniques with experienced mediators.

In today's world it is likely that even lawyers who are not litigators are aware of the widespread use of mediation. It is also likely that most experienced litigators have represented clients in mediations, the most common form of what has historically been termed "Alternative Dispute

Resolution" (ADR). Mediation has proven to be the ADR process of choice for most attorneys. Therefore, this book will focus on mediation but will also include brief discussions of arbitration, special masters and early neutral evaluation since these processes may sometimes lead to mediation.

The principal benefit of mediation is that it is a "time out" in the litigation process involving assisted negotiation, a "break" that allows the parties to control their own destinies. A very high percentage of cases are settled at mediation and even if some are not successfully concluded, the stage is set for further discussions that frequently lead to a settlement.

As a result of my experiences in representing clients in mediations, and serving as a mediator, I have become a true believer in the process. I have seen how "making peace" at mediation, rather than "making war" at trial, benefited clients because they could control their own destinies and reach a resolution that they, not strangers in a jury box, decided made sense. In my representation of clients in mediations, I never heard one say, "I am sorry the case is over. I really wish I had gone to trial."

I know that some lawyers do not share my enthusiasm for mediation. Nevertheless, mediation is not the wave of the future, but rather a wave that has crested and come ashore. Whether lawyers like mediation, are lukewarm about it, or don't like it, it is here to stay. No matter one's personal view, it is my hope that this book will provide some practical and useful observations and recommendations for those who represent clients in mediations.

Ken Shigley, a past-president of the State Bar of Georgia, observed at a continuing legal education program that in today's world, trials, not mediations, have become the alternative way to resolve cases. This observation demonstrates why "Dispute Resolution" (DR) has replaced "Alternative Dispute Resolution" (ADR) in the terminology of many professional organizations, professional practices, and continuing legal education programs and presentations.

OBSERVATIONS ON TRIALS

"Discourage litigation. Persuade your neighbors to compromise whenever you can. Point out to them that the nominal winner is often a real loser, in fees, expenses, and waste of time. As a peace maker the lawyer has a superior opportunity of being a good man. There will still be business enough."

Abraham Lincoln
"Notes for a Law Lecture"

"Why would they want twelve strangers or six strangers, as the case might be, deciding these big complex disputes? And why would they think they'd be better served than in a settlement? I've always preached that settlement is the best form of justice."

Anthony A. Alaimo
U.S. District Court Judge,
Southern District of Georgia

"Only a very foolish lawyer will dare guess the outcome of a jury trial."

> Jerome Frank
> Judge, United States Court of Appeals,
> Second Circuit

"I have never met a litigator who did not think he was winning the case right up to the moment when the guillotine came down."

> William F. Baxter
> Assistant U.S. Attorney General

"But juries are not bound by what seems inescapable logic to judges."

> Robert H. Jackson
> Associate Justice, United States Supreme Court

"The jury has the power to bring in a verdict in the teeth of both law and facts."

> Oliver Wendell Holmes
> Associate Justice, United States Supreme Court

"A jury verdict is a quotient of the prejudices of twelve people."

> Kenneth P. Grubb
> American Jurist

"When you go into court you are putting your fate in the hands of twelve people who weren't smart enough to get out of jury duty."

Norm Crosby
Comedian

"Only two things can happen at trial and one of them is bad."

A. Rowland Dye
Noted Trial Lawyer

Chapter 1

SUCCESS AT MEDIATION – WHAT IS IT?

"You can't always get what you want;
You can't always get what you want;
But if you try sometimes,
You just might find, You get what you need."

MICK JAGGER AND KEITH RICHARDS

Why does this book start off discussing success at mediation by asking what is success? Attorneys experienced in representing clients in mediations know that succeeding and "winning" are not the same thing. You win (or lose) at trial. You succeed at mediation by achieving results that are in the best interests of your clients. In accomplishing this goal, your clients control their own destiny, achieve a certainty of result, and bring their case to a conclusion much sooner than in a trial which, more often than not, will occur at some unknown time in the future. And what if there is an appeal? Furthermore, your clients control legal expenses, and if confidentiality is important, it is often possible to secure an agreement in which the terms of a settlement will remain confidential.

Success does not mean your clients getting everything they want. That seldom happens. But there is great value in eliminating risks and anxieties that are inherent in all trials.

"Success" has been defined as, "The accomplishment of an aim or purpose" (Oxford Dictionaries) and "the favorable outcome of something attempted" (The Free Dictionary). Concluding a case on terms decided by your client, with your professional guidance, constitutes real success.

Chapter 2

WHY ALL LAWYERS SHOULD BE FAMILIAR WITH MEDIATION

"The very first step towards success in any occupation is to become interested in it."

WILLIAM OSLER

Why should lawyers who don't litigate know anything about mediation? Isn't mediation something only litigators need to know about? In today's world the answer is "no" for lawyers of all areas of practice who are unlikely to ever see the inside of a courtroom: business, wills and estates, employment, bankruptcy, real estate, construction, workers' compensation and every other area of law.

The odds are great that at some point in their careers, non-litigators will either advise clients in matters that appear likely to lead to litigation or, when litigation begins, that a client will seek their advice. For the non-litigator, showing knowledge of a cost-saving way to deal with disputes, and assisting with a cost-benefit analysis of possible or actual litigation, will impress clients and increase confidence that their lawyer is looking out for them. In order to counsel their clients satisfactorily, all lawyers should know something about mediation.

Additionally, in certain matters it may be helpful for a non-litigator to assist at a mediation because of his or her specialized or historical knowledge pertinent to the dispute. When this situation exists, it will be important for the non-litigator to understand how mediation works.

Further, mediation involves negotiation seeking to reach an acceptable result for clients, and non-litigators routinely negotiate on behalf of their clients in many different types of legal matters. Attorneys who don't litigate cases could find themselves participating in the negotiating process at a mediation involving one of their clients along with the litigator handling the case. This has occurred in cases I have mediated.

Non-litigators who know about and understand the benefits of mediation can help clients save time and money by ending a dispute or lawsuit in such a way that their clients decide was in their best interests.

Chapter 3

FIRST SOME BASICS:

*"The courts of this country should not be the
places where resolution of disputes begins.
They should be the places where the disputes
end and after alternative methods of
resolving disputes have been considered and tried."*

SANDRA DAY O'CONNOR

At its heart, mediation is assisted negotiation. It is a private, confidential, and informal process that provides an alternative to a judge or jury deciding the outcome of a legal dispute. It is conciliatory, where compromise is necessarily involved, rather than adversarial, where one side wins and the other loses.

Very importantly, what occurs in a mediation is confidential. If the case does not get resolved, because mediations involve settlement negotiations, no judge or jury may be presented evidence on what parties or counsel either said or did. All a judge may be told is that the case did or did not settle, subject to the limited exceptions to confidentiality discussed in Chapter 23.

What does "assisted negotiation" mean? It means that discussions concerning the case, and a means for its resolution, are guided by the mediator. The goal of the process is that the parties reach a decision that is a satisfactory resolution of their dispute. How a mediator can assist in accomplishing this will be discussed in some detail in Chapter 19.

Most importantly, in mediation the parties control their case. Because of court procedures and rules of evidence, no judge or jury will ever know as much about their case as they and their lawyers do. At mediation, clients, with advice from their lawyers, decide if the case will be resolved and how. Even where mediation is court-ordered, the parties are not required to reach a settlement. If they want their day in court they shall have it.

Because the mediation process is informal, there are no required procedures or rules of evidence to be followed. Parties don't testify. Their lawyers can do all of the talking. They don't have to say anything if they don't want to, and if they do speak, they will not be cross-examined.

Despite the lack of formal procedure, a mediation most often begins with a joint session in which the parties, or their representatives, and their counsel are present. In some instances, however, the mediator or the parties may believe that an initial joint session should not be held, especially if there are hard feelings or emotions that run high. In such situations, the mediator begins by conducting individual private meetings, commonly referred to as caucuses.

When there is an initial joint session, the mediator commonly begins by explaining the mediation process and its benefits, focusing on those who have not previously participated in a mediation. Counsel are then invited to make presentations in which they express their views of the case based upon the facts and the law they rely on. Sometimes presentations may not be made and something like, "We are all very familiar with this case and I don't need to make a presentation and we are ready to move into the private caucuses" is what may be said. Some presentations, however, may be detailed and lengthy, particularly in complex cases. A client, or client's representative, may or may not choose to make remarks. Following the joint session, the mediator will conduct separate private meetings with the parties and their counsel; at this point the negotiations begin and will continue throughout the mediation.

In an initial private meeting, the mediator typically asks if there is any confidential information that the mediator should be aware of that was not presented in the joint session. Another typical question is, "What do you believe are the most important points to discuss with the other side?" As the process continues in subsequent private meetings, the mediator will continue to ask questions about the case and the parties' positions. "Shuttle diplomacy" occurs as the mediator presents each side's views and positions while also communicating demands, offers, counter-demands and counter-offers.

Most mediations begin, and may continue, as what is known as "facilitative mediation," an approach that some mediators use exclusively either because of personal philosophy or sometimes rules of a jurisdiction. In purely facilitative mediation, the mediator does not directly express opinions about positions, provide analysis, or discuss possible outcomes. Rather, the mediator engages the parties in discussions to help them assess their risks and focus on their interests. While doing this, however, the mediator may sometimes play devil's advocate and set forth an alternative position for the sake of argument, both to encourage discussion and enable counsel and parties to examine possible weaknesses in their positions. The mediator may also assist the parties in thinking about settlement options. And, when it appears there may be an impasse, there are approaches the mediator may take to help the parties work through it.

On occasion, either at the request of the parties, or if the mediator believes it could assist in reaching a settlement, the mediator may engage in "evaluative mediation" to one degree or another, and express opinions regarding the case. It should be noted that within the mediation profession there are those who believe engaging in evaluative mediation is never proper because doing so impinges on the core principle of mediation: "self-determination," *i.e.*, that a party's decision to settle or not is theirs and theirs alone and should not be influenced by the mediator. Additionally, some courts prohibit a mediator's expression of opinions while others have permitted it. If a mediator does provide some form of evaluation, it is essential to avoid giving an opinion too soon. The danger is that a party may believe that the mediator is taking sides and not remaining impartial. In evaluative mediation the mediator should not control what parties do but may still choose to express opinions on the merits of the case, its risks and potential outcomes. The mediator may sometimes recommend a settlement range or make a specific settlement proposal while providing his or her thoughts as to why agreeing to a settlement could be in a party's best interests. As always, however, the parties are not required to accept any evaluation or settle based upon it.

Formal and informal surveys have revealed that a majority of lawyers often want mediators to evaluate at some point during a mediation. Today, many mediators will do so when requested so long as it is not prohibited in the jurisdiction involved and if they believe it will help the parties reach a settlement that they, not the mediator, decide is in their best interests.

Although some mediations may only last a few hours, it is not unusual for mediations to last much or all of the day, sometimes they may last more than one. Occasionally, two or more mediation sessions may occur. The success rate for reaching a settlement at mediation is high. Even if an agreement is not reached, however, mediation often leads to further discussions that result in a settlement.

When a settlement is reached, it is customary for a mediator to work with the attorneys in setting out its essential terms in a mediation settlement agreement memorandum. The agreement is signed by the parties, their attorneys and the mediator in his or her capacity as the neutral involved. In this document it is agreed that the formal settlement documents (*e.g.*, releases, dismissals, etc.) will be prepared soon thereafter. Examples of basic mediation settlement agreement memoranda forms are set out in Appendices D and E.

Chapter 4

WHY DOES MEDIATION WORK?

"The only difference between stumbling blocks and
stepping stones is how you use them."

ADRIANA DOYLE

Settlement statistics for mediated cases have generally been reported as 80% and sometimes even higher. Something about the mediation process results in "success."

As mentioned earlier, "making peace, not war" is the purpose of this process. It creates an environment that helps cut through counter-productive adversarial actions as the parties work with the mediator, and the mediator works with them, in developing and reaching what the parties decide is a mutually acceptable compromise.

In mediations no side is likely to get everything it wants. Yet, the parties, more often than not, will reach a point where rational thought tells them they should not turn down a possible deal that is in their best interests because of the uncertainties and risks inherent in a trial.

Mediation provides the unique opportunity to get decision makers and their lawyers together at one time, in one location, where full attention can be devoted to the legal dispute involved. On such a day, those who need to focus on resolving the case can do so.

Mediation also provides a confidential environment in which parties can share their goals and concerns with the mediator. As a result, the mediator has the opportunity to assist in controlling and directing discussions and negotiations in a positive way. If a mediator is asked to keep certain information that is shared confidential, he or she will do so.

During the mediation, posturing, if not totally eliminated, is commonly reduced as negotiations proceed. As a result, the parties move from focusing on their legal and factual positions to their interests in ending their legal dispute.

As a mediation progresses, the parties normally become more realistic in their expectations. "Advocacy bias," the natural tendency of parties and their lawyers to perceive their side of the case as stronger than it may actually be, often begins to fade. The same occurs with respect to assessments of settlement value. Chapter 18 discusses common psychological barriers that may get in the way of achieving success. The mediator, through techniques discussed later in Chapter 19, helps the parties deal with these and overcome unrealistic expectations.

Mediation allows the parties "to hear each other" either directly, through the mediator, or both. Even if they don't agree with what the other side is saying, they typically gain some understanding of why the opposite party is taking its position.

Mediation is flexible. It provides the opportunity to craft solutions that a judge or jury cannot: in serious personal injury cases one may be a structured settlement; in business disputes, an agreement for future mutually beneficial business arrangements; in employment cases, an apology and the opportunity to work in another department. The solution is in the hands of those who will know more about their dispute than a judge or jury ever will.

And, to emphasize an earlier point, even if a settlement is not reached on the day of the mediation, the process frequently sets the stage for further settlement discussions because it gets the parties talking. More often than not, these discussions lead to a settlement.

Why does mediation work? Because it brings the decision makers together, decreases posturing, forces the decision makers to focus on their interests, results in more realistic case assessments, and provides flexibility in achieving a result that is mutually beneficial.

Chapter 5

WHY MEDIATE?

"If we don't change the direction we are going,
we will end up where we are heading."

CHINESE PROVERB

As the quotes cited earlier in "Observations On Trials" reflect, the most important reason to mediate a legal dispute is to provide clients the opportunity to control their own destinies and achieve certainty of outcome. It has sometimes been observed that even a client with a "slam-dunk" case still has a ten percent chance of losing in a jury trial. This may or may not be true, but, lawyers who have tried enough cases, if being candid, will likely tell you they won cases they doubted they would win (either the verdict on liability or the amount of damages awarded) and lost cases they didn't think they would lose (also the verdict on liability or the amount of damages awarded). And these outcomes may not have been the result of exceptional, or unexceptional, skills. The "luck of the draw" in getting a jury that misunderstands or ignores the facts, the law, or both, is a factor.

Early in my career, a very experienced and highly regarded trial lawyer told me, "Ray, when you go to trial only two things can happen and one of them is bad." One should pause before entrusting his or her fate to those unpredictable strangers in the jury box.

Plaintiffs and defendants should mediate for the same reasons. The most important of these are to control one's destiny, eliminate risk, and achieve certainty of result.

No judge or jury will ever know as much about a case as the parties and their lawyers. Because of limitations of time, the formalities of court, and strict rules of evidence, even the most conscientious judge and jury won't have the same knowledge as the parties and their lawyers do. Mediation provides the opportunity to make rational decisions based upon the knowledge the parties and their lawyers possess but a judge or jury will never have.

Mediation allows a client to talk to someone other than their lawyer about their case and, for some, this is psychologically important. Even though a mediator is not a judge, and can't make anyone do anything, in the eyes of a client it is not uncommon for a mediator to be seen as an authority figure who listens and understands the way they feel about the case or legal dispute they are involved in.

Mediation is much less stressful than a trial. I never met a client who looked forward to testifying and being cross examined. Nor have I ever met a client, or lawyer for that matter, who looked forward to waiting for a jury to deliberate, return to the courtroom and announce its verdict. Even the most experienced lawyers get butterflies in their stomachs at that point. Think how a client must feel.

Some have said that settlement at mediation is a "win/win" result. I am not sure that is accurate. A settlement may, in fact, be a "no-lose/no-lose" outcome that simply makes sense.

Experienced lawyers know that the vast majority of cases settle prior to going to trial. The question most often becomes not if a case will settle, but when. Why not try to achieve a settlement sooner rather than later? Mediation provides the opportunity to do so resulting in cost savings for a client that are both direct and indirect. Direct costs include attorney fees and expenses of litigation. Even when a case is taken on a contingent fee basis, litigation expenses may be substantial. Indirect costs for a client may include emotional ones, as well as "distraction" costs interfering with day to day activities or responsibilities.

In summary, the reasons to mediate are:

* Control of one's own destiny.
* Certainty of result.
* Elimination of risk.
* Speed of resolution.
* Cost savings.
* Confidentiality.
* Avoiding the stress and anxiety of going to trial.
* If not achieving a "win-win" result, at least achieving a "no-lose/ no-lose" one.
* Setting the stage for further discussions if the case does not settle at the mediation.

Lastly, perhaps there is one more reason. Upon occasion a client may get more, or give up less, than they expected. While not being all that common, it has happened in cases in which I represented clients, as well as, (when some tell me afterwards) in cases I mediated.

Chapter 6

WHEN TO MEDIATE?

"Timing has a lot to do with the outcome of a rain dance."

COWBOY PROVERB

With the reasons to mediate set out in Chapter 5 in mind, when is the right time to do so? There is no hard and fast rule. It will vary depending upon the circumstances of any given case or legal dispute. The right time depends upon the parties' belief that there is sufficient information to make decisions that are in their best interests. Most mediations will occur when sufficient discovery has been completed for the parties to more realistically assess their positions, risks and the possible outcomes of a trial. That being said, in many instances, sooner, rather than later is best for clients because costs are reduced and a settlement permits them to end their uncertainties, anxieties and concerns resulting from litigation.

In certain business or employment disputes, it may be appropriate to mediate prior to or soon after the filing of a lawsuit. The same may be true for tort cases involving clear, or highly likely, liability where damages can be readily evaluated. When pre-litigation mediation occurs, if the dispute is resolved, substantial legal expenses will be saved. The same holds true for lawsuits which have been filed but may be promptly mediated with little or no discovery being necessary. In more complex cases, voluntary mediation is most likely to be successful after there has been sufficient discovery for the parties to realistically assess their strengths and weaknesses and the risks of going to trial.

It is not unusual for a mediation to be court-ordered with or without a date by which it must be completed specified. Many judges have come to believe mediation is in the best interests of both the litigants and the courts. These judges know a successful mediation will relieve them from devoting time to a case which is more likely than not to settle once a trial date draws near.

It is best to avoid mediation on the eve of trial. If the case cannot be resolved, it is important that there be sufficient time to react to what may be learned at a mediation about the need for additional discovery, filing of motions or further case preparation. Following this process increases the likelihood that, ultimately, the case will be settled and that there will be no need to go to trial.

Chapter 7

WHO SHOULD MEDIATE?

"Why not go out on a limb? Isn't that where the fruit is?"

FRANK SCULLY

This is the shortest chapter in this book. Who should mediate? Any person or business involved in any type of legal dispute should be open to mediation because of the benefits discussed in Chapter 5. Mediation has been successfully used in personal injury and wrongful death actions, business and contract disputes, employment disputes, professional negligence cases, construction cases, insurance cases, and virtually every other type of civil litigation, including domestic relations cases involving division of property and child custody issues.

Anyone wishing to end a legal dispute so as to limit the time, expense, risks, uncertainty and anxiety involved in litigation should mediate because mediation is the most effective way to accomplish these goals.

Chapter 8

CHOOSING YOUR MEDIATOR

*"One of the most important factors within your control
which will increase the odds of a successful mediation is
the selection of the mediator....Patience is a virtue, and the
most important quality an effective mediator will possess"*

HON. JOHN P. DIBLASI

There are two principal philosophies for selecting a mediator. One is to select a mediator with expertise in a particular subject matter. A second is to select a mediator known by counsel to possess key skills discussed below and who can quickly grasp the important aspects of the case. Those adhering to the second philosophy believe a "quick study" will be able to review pre-mediation submissions and, at the mediation, obtain a sufficient grasp of the case to assist in its resolution.

After my many years of representing clients in mediations, I concluded that the "quick study" mediator with a history of a varied litigation practice and the experience to be able to grasp the essentials of a case, is most often the best choice. Of course, there are always exceptions.

Where highly technical or very specialized issues are involved, as in patent litigation, complex construction disputes, and engineering cases, expertise is important. However, in many cases, a mediator who listens to discussions of the evidence and legal arguments, and can help with "reality checks" which may result in parties concluding a position or belief is not realistic, is most useful.

Key skills and qualities to look for in a mediator include:

1) The ability to be empathetic and develop rapport with participants in the mediation, *i.e.*, having a good "bedside manner."
2) Persistence. Not giving up too soon. Patience.
3) The ability to be direct with clients and counsel when helpful.
4) The ability to provide meaningful "reality checks" about a case and the risks of what might happen at trial.
5) Skills as a facilitator who is also willing to "evaluate" when asked or when believed helpful, subject to limitations or prohibitions as discussed in Chapter 19.
6) Experience to know when there should be a "lawyers only meeting."
7) The ability and willingness to assist in continuing negotiations when the case doesn't settle.

No matter which philosophy for selecting a mediator you subscribe to, even if it is the one in which expertise is most important, make certain you choose one with the skills and qualities set out above.

Finally, as observed by an anonymous mediator in response to a survey, there is a particular skill that can be key to assisting parties reach a successful resolution:

"I think the greatest and most useful skill I have is the ability to gain people's trust. They come to believe that I will not lie or mislead them and what I am interested in reaching is a settlement that works for them."

Chapter 9

COURT-ORDERED MEDIATION:

WHY IT IS A GOOD THING

"A pessimist sees difficulty in every opportunity;
an optimist sees opportunity in every difficulty."

WINSTON CHURCHILL

O bviously, participation in court-ordered mediation is not voluntary, whether or not your client agrees to settle the case is. The
difference between court-ordered and voluntary mediation is how you
get there. Once you are there, the process is the same.

Court-ordered mediation has become increasingly widespread.
Even where not required in a particular jurisdiction, individual judges
may order it for many, or even all, civil cases on their docket.

Why do judges like court-ordered mediation? They know most cases
settle. They don't like calling potential jurors in for cases that settle on
the courthouse steps resulting in nothing to try or which settle during a
trial, and for those potential or actual jurors to come away believing that
their time has been wasted. Furthermore, and importantly, a successful

mediation can eliminate the need for a judge to spend time on motions and other pre-trial matters for cases that will settle. Judges know that a court-ordered mediation will at least get the parties talking. They are also aware of the significant expense involved in preparing cases for trial and trying them and that all parties will benefit if these expenses can be avoided.

Some lawyers don't like court-ordered mediation while other lawyers do. Those who dislike them usually say that an opposing party may not come with a serious intent to settle, or that the opposing party is only going to go through the motions, or that the opposing party will only use the process to figure out a trial strategy. Sometimes these objections may be valid, but in my experience as counsel and mediator, they are quite rare. Most court-ordered mediations I have been involved in have resulted in settlements.

Those who like court-ordered mediation typically state two reasons. First, since most cases settle, there is an earlier opportunity for settlement to occur. Even if the case does not settle the day of mediation, the stage is set for further settlement discussions that frequently succeed. Secondly, although some lawyers believe that suggesting mediation will be perceived as a sign of weakness, they are still convinced that mediation is in the best interest of their client. A court ordered mediation eliminates the "sign of weakness" fear.

My personal experience as counsel with court-ordered mediations in federal and state courts was quite positive. If I were a judge I would require mediation. As counsel, I would welcome it.

Chapter 10

PREPARING YOURSELF FOR MEDIATION

*"If you don't know where you are going
you will end up some place else."*

YOGI BERRA

It is just as important to prepare yourself for mediation as it is to prepare yourself for trial. This preparation requires a number of different elements to be taken into consideration. First, as discussed earlier, it is important to pick the right time to mediate. There may be an occasion for pre-suit or early stage mediation, but more often than not, it will occur after a lawsuit has been filed and at least some discovery conducted. Make sure sufficient information has been developed to understand the true strengths and weaknesses of your client's case on both liability and damages. As a rule of thumb, although you may not have completed all the discovery you would like, you should be at the point where you are prepared to go to trial if you should need to. This rule is a good one to follow except when liability and damages are not being seriously disputed and you are dealing with a "how much is it going to take" case.

Second, it is important to select a mediator who is good with people, especially in personal injury cases. A good "bedside manner" is very helpful in dealing with emotional plaintiffs who are unfamiliar with the judicial process. Pick a mediator who is trusted and respected by your opponent. I frequently asked the lawyer on the other side of a case I was handling to suggest potential mediators. So long as you believe one of those suggested will be fair and realistic, agree to the choice. Since it will be more difficult for your opponent to reject what the suggested mediator says and does in guiding mediation settlement negotiations, this strategy can prove to be very helpful. If you represent a defendant, consider a mediator who has done some plaintiff's work. If you represent a plaintiff, consider a mediator who has done some defense work. Again, your mediator's experience "on the same side of the fence" as your opponent can make it more difficult for your opponent to reject what the mediator says and does. Of course, it is essential that you believe that the mediator will be fair and realistic no matter what side of the professional fence he or she comes from. Chapter 8 discusses selection of a mediator in greater detail.

Third, establish the right mindset. If your goal is to leave the mediation with your client's case settled, you will need a different mindset from the one you would bring to a trial. At trial, mindsets are necessarily adversarial. Lawyers go to trial to "make war." With mediation, however, while still being adversaries, lawyers should adopt a "conflict resolution" mindset, one where the goal is to "make peace."

Admittedly, the transition into a "make peace" mindset can be difficult. It is unrealistic to expect that an advocate can totally put aside an adversarial one. Still, to achieve a settlement in the best interests of a client, controlling that mindset is important.

This does not mean being too soft or conceding more than is appropriate. Remain firm and drive a hard bargain. But remember, the goal is to get that bargain. A cooperative, conciliatory and rational attitude is important for a successful result; however, showing that you are ready and willing to try the case if a fair settlement cannot be reached is just as important.

In preparing for mediation, it is important to think about how mediators go about their job. As discussed in Chapter 3, most mediations involve the mediators explaining the mediation process for the benefit of the party or parties who do not have mediation experience. This explanation is followed by inviting the plaintiff's counsel to make a presentation which, in turn, is followed by inviting the defendant's counsel to do the same. Sometimes, however, counsel may decide not to make presentations. When presentations are made, the mediator may invite brief rebuttals. In preparing your presentation, it is important to anticipate what your opponent will say and to be prepared, if necessary, to point to facts and/or law which undercuts your opponent's position.

In the joint session the mediator may ask questions of one or both sides about points they have made that might need some clarification in order to assist in the process. Be prepared for that. Customarily, the joint session will be followed by private caucuses with each side in which your mediator typically asks questions that seek an explanation of some of your key points. It is also likely questions will be asked about what your opponent has said and your response. Be prepared for this questioning as "reality testing" is all part of the mediator's job. This process may involve open-ended and non-judgmental questions to get you and your client to think about potential areas of difficulty in the case. For example, "I heard your opposing counsel say that there was an eyewitness supporting his version of the case. Can you help me with that?" Or, "How strong do you think your opponent really believes her case is and why would she believe that?" The process may involve questions about when and where the case will be tried, whether any motions have been filed and their status, and if you have information on any jury verdicts or settlements in similar cases. You can also expect questions about your judge and what type of jurors are likely.

Anticipate that your mediator may ask "reality testing" questions such as:

To the plaintiff, "If you won what do you believe the range of the verdict could be?"

To the defendant, "If you lost what do you believe the range of the verdict could be?"

"What do you think your opponent and his/her client believe are their strengths and why do you think they believe that?"

"What do you think your opponent and his/her client believe are your weaknesses and why do you think they believe that?"

Be prepared to answer these questions or ones like them. The mediator's purpose is to get you to think about your case's actual or potential weaknesses and to gauge your response. A more detailed discussion of what mediators do and why is found in Chapter 19.

A side note: be aware that a mediator may not accept your answers as totally candid. As one mediator once said to me in a private caucus, "I get lied to every day." Mediators expect posturing.

In most cases, be prepared to move away from arguing the facts and the law to the mediator after the first two or three private caucuses. In many cases such arguments are not necessary. Rather, focus on your client's interests and concerns. Ultimately, the mediator's job is a practical one - to help you get the case settled. Consequently, he or she will need to deal with money and any other factors important to the parties. The focus becomes an exchange of demands, offers, counter-demands and counter-offers, and not unnecessary repetitive pronouncements about the justness of your client's case.

You must also be aware of "advocacy bias," an attitude common to all advocates. As you enter into the mediation, recognize that, as much as you would like to believe that you are being totally objective in evaluating your client's case, you cannot be. It is likely that you will believe your chance of winning at trial is better than it is. It is also likely you may be convinced that a damages award will be more (if you represent the plaintiff) or less (if you represent the defendant) than is realistic. Chapter 18 includes a more detailed discussion of the psychological aspects of mediation.

In mediations it is a common saying that a good settlement has occurred when both sides walk away unhappy. Although this is not always the case, be prepared to walk away a bit "unhappy" when the settlement which is possible makes sense for your client.

Chapter 11

PREPARING YOUR CLIENT FOR MEDIATION

*"The greatest trust between man and man
is the trust of giving counsel."*

FRANCIS BACON

U nless your client is a defendant who does not personally attend but, has an experienced claims adjuster, or other representative instead, it is unlikely that he or she will have any experience in mediations. It is important that you explain what mediation is, what it isn't, and how the process works. At the same time, discuss your assessment of the strengths and weaknesses of your client's case and the risks involved in going to trial. The mediator will almost certainly discuss these topics in some fashion, whether directly or indirectly, in a private caucus. You don't want your client to hear your assessment of weaknesses and risks for the first time in a private caucus.

In explaining what mediation is, you should help your client clearly understand that it is a very different procedure from a trial. This knowledge will help reduce your client's anxiety level. One way to explain the difference is to tell a client that at a trial you intend "to make war" while at mediation your goal is "to make peace." Let your client know that because of this difference you will be firm but will not engage in unnecessary adversarial behavior because doing so would be detrimental to the goal of reaching a settlement that is in his or her best interest.

Explain that mediation is an informal process and that the mediator is not a judge who decides winner and loser. Explain that a mediator does not take sides but remains neutral with the goal of helping the case get settled.

Discuss mediation procedure. Unless there is some reason an initial joint session should not occur, explain that after the mediator's opening remarks, attorneys for each side normally make brief comments or presentations while everyone is together. A client's anxiety is reduced when he/she understands that he/she will not be testifying or undergoing cross-examination. Let your client know it is not necessary to speak at all, although on occasion it may be helpful to do so, and that you will review the pros and cons before a final decision is made. Advise your client that if it would be helpful to say something, you will give advice as to what should be said and how best to say it.

Even if your client will not speak in the joint session, however, you should prepare him or her to respond to questions the mediator may ask. Explain that after the initial joint session, the mediator will likely ask questions about the strong and weak points of the case during separate private meetings. Let your client know that the mediator may play "devil's advocate" in an effort to assist the parties with a more objective analysis of their case. It does not mean the mediator is taking sides. Tell your client that when you discuss any weaknesses or concerns with the mediator, you will not be "caving in" but, instead, working with the mediator to resolve the case in a favorable but realistic way. Let your client know the mediator will agree to keep such discussions confidential when you make such a request.

Explain your reasons for believing that mediation is a good idea:

1) Control - mediation allows clients to be in control of their own destiny. They, and not a judge or strangers on a jury, will determine the outcome.
2) Certainty - what will happen at trial, or in an appeal, is never certain. Even if there is a good result at trial, an appeal could bring a reversal and the need to try the case again.
3) Time - if successful, mediation will obtain resolution of the case sooner rather than later – there will be no need to wait for a trial date or result of any appeal.
4) Costs - mediation reduces total costs associated with further case preparation, trial and possible appeal.
5) Confidentiality - matters that clients desire to be kept private will not be subject to public disclosure as they would in a trial. It may also be possible to keep the terms of a settlement confidential if that is important.
6) Time value of money - for a plaintiff, resolving the case more quickly results in a known amount of money being available almost immediately rather than an uncertain amount at some unknown point in the future.

Let your client know that the process may be a lengthy one while demands and counter-demands, offers and counter-offers are exchanged. Explain that the mediator will be engaging in "shuttle diplomacy," going back and forth between each side. The client should also understand that at times, it will appear nothing is happening while the mediator meets with the other side, or when the other side may be engaged in private discussions outside the presence of the mediator.

If you represent a plaintiff inexperienced in mediations, advise him or her that your first demand will be for substantially more than you know the defendant is willing to pay. Conversely, if you represent a defendant inexperienced in mediations, your first offer will be for sub-stantially less than what you believe it will take to settle the case. If you represent the plaintiff, explain that your goal is to get the defendant to pay the most he/she/it is willing to pay. If you represent the defendant, explain that your goal is to get the plaintiff to take the least he/she/it is willing to take. To help your client better understand what is happen-ing, you may wish to say that what you are doing is "playing poker" to get the other side's final demand or offer on the table to see if that will settle the case.

Let your client know that as hard as lawyers and clients may try, it is difficult to be totally objective. Therefore, it is important to keep an open mind and work with, and listen to, what the mediator says even if you don't agree with it.

Explain that what occurs at a successful mediation is a compromise where no side gets everything it wants. Instead, both sides decide that a settlement should be agreed to when it makes sense because it is in their best interests. Accordingly, patience is necessary even when there may be times both of you get frustrated, and may want to leave because you believe the other side is being unreasonable. However, you should tell your client that so long as the mediator asks you to stay, you will do so be-cause you trust the mediator to tell you if there is no point in continuing.

In advising a plaintiff it is important to talk about appropriate at-tire and not wearing excessive or flashy jewelry (and in today's world, covering tattoos as much as possible, not to mention dealing with body piercings). Also, that he or she should be polite at all times and make an effort to appear congenial and likeable.

Furthermore, if you represent a plaintiff in a personal injury case, explain that payments for personal injury are not taxable. In a cata-strophic injury or wrongful death case, it may be appropriate to talk about the possibility and advantages of a structured settlement, *i.e.*, long-term financial protection and tax advantages. If you represent an insured defendant, the carrier will be aware of the potential advantage of using structured settlements in an effort to make settlement offers more attractive to a plaintiff.

In summary, when preparing clients it is important to have them understand why you believe mediation is beneficial. It is also important that clients understand how mediations work because they will then be more inclined to believe that you know what you are doing.

Chapter 12

PREPARING YOUR MEDIATOR FOR MEDIATION

"I passionately believe that it's not just what you say that counts, it's also how you say it – that the success of your argument critically depends on your manner of presenting it."

ALAIN DE BOTTON

A mediator does not represent any party in a legal dispute. A mediator's only "client" is the settlement. Help your mediator represent this "client." Your mediator is being paid to assist you and your opponent settle the case, and he/she will be disappointed if the process does not result in a settlement.

Many mediators ask for written submissions prior to mediation but some may not. You should provide one even if your mediator does not. In cases that are not complex, a letter or email may be sufficient while others may require more detail. Outline your client's case as you see it. Support it by key facts and, where necessary, applicable law. Point out the strengths of your side of the case and the weaknesses in your opponent's. This submission may be a confidential communication, *i.e.*, not to be shared with your opponent. (But more on providing information to your opponent in Chapter 13.)

Preparing your mediator in advance, rather than simply relying on a presentation at the initial joint session, is often helpful. It may be difficult for your mediator to absorb everything you believe is important based solely upon your oral presentation.

You may decide that your written submission should include not only your version of the facts and the law but also attachments such as excerpts from depositions, copies of key documents or photographs, copies of key cases, etc. If you provide these, highlighting the parts you rely on will be helpful to the mediator.

It is important that what you submit comes across as explanatory and credible. You want to impress the mediator as being rational and reasonable. If your materials don't convey that impression, the mediator may discount what you provide and wonder about what you say in the joint session and private caucuses.

In preparing your mediator, you may want to suggest a conference call with counsel for the parties during which the mediator can be briefed on the positions of the parties, anticipated problems that will need to be worked through, procedural matters, etc. Depending on the nature of the case, and the professional working relationship of counsel, this may be a very useful step. You may also want to request private telephone calls with your mediator in advance of the mediation. These can be particularly helpful when you want to share confidential information concerning unreasonable expectations by your client or other sensitive matters you believe would be helpful for the mediator to know about. I believe, however, that it is important for counsel to agree that such calls are permissible to avoid any concern of unfair ex parte "lobbying."

Remember, the better prepared your mediator is in understanding the facts and the law that support your case, the better your mediator will be able to assist in guiding settlement negotiations in a meaningful and efficient way.

Chapter 13

PREPARING YOUR OPPONENT FOR MEDIATION

"It is impossible to defeat an ignorant man in an argument."

WILLIAM GIBBS McADOO

S uggesting that you prepare your opponent for mediation may cause you to ask, "What? Are you crazy? Why would I want to prepare my opponent?" However, such preparation is important when your opponent sincerely desires to settle the case. Setting out the facts and the law that support your case, and providing these in advance of the mediation, make it more likely that information you believe is important for the other side to consider in its settlement evaluation will be reviewed.

Some attorneys believe that if they provide information about their case to opponents, their opponents will be better prepared if the case goes to trial. Two comments on that: first, virtually all civil cases settle without going to trial, and second, if there is a competent lawyer opposing you, he or she will likely be aware of your strong points prior to trial. When competent lawyers are involved, by the time a case goes to trial there are few secrets. How often have you experienced, or even heard of, a trial where a "Perry Mason moment" resulted in victory? Holding back may only result in a minimal tactical advantage that, in reality, will have little impact on the outcome of a trial. So why not have your strong points factored into your opponent's settlement analysis?

Educating the other side on the strengths of your case, its weaknesses, and the hurdles it will face at trial, allows a thorough analysis that will help your opponent come to mediation with a realistic settlement position. A goal is to help reduce your opponent's "advocacy bias" in advance rather than leaving it to your mediator to deal with for the first time. Allow time for what your opponent does not want to hear, or accept, to sink in prior to the mediation.

Providing information helps decision makers evaluate a case and can be helpful to your opposing counsel in getting a client to a realistic settlement position. Your goal in educating the other side is to reduce the risk of forming unrealistic expectations which will make mediation negotiations more difficult and, perhaps, make a settlement impossible.

Remember, for mediations, the purpose of preparing opponents is to persuade them to move to settlement positions they really do not want to.

Chapter 14

MEDIATION ADVOCACY

"Use soft words and hard arguments."

ENGLISH PROVERB

Mediation advocacy is fundamentally different from trial advocacy. It is a blend of presentation, discussion and negotiation.

My experiences have taught me that there are at least five stages of mediation advocacy:

* Pre-mediation advocacy.
* At the beginning – the joint session.
* During – the private caucuses and, possibly, private meetings with your opposing counsel.
* Near the end when an apparent impasse has been reached.
* After the mediation session when an agreement has not been reached but there is a willingness to keep talking.

In the early days of mediation, it was not unusual for counsel to make the same type of adversarial presentation common to opening and closing arguments at trial. Even today, lawyers not experienced in mediating cases may take this approach. Rather than contributing to reaching a mutually beneficial settlement, however, this approach often results in a hardening of positions that makes reaching a settlement more difficult.

Experienced mediators agree that "make peace not war" mindsets and presentations are very important. This guiding principle does not mean you should not be a strong and firm advocate for your client. You should be. Drive a hard bargain, but remember that the goal of your advocacy is to resolve the case. Insulting comments, "fighting words" or a "slash and burn" approach inevitably make resolution much more difficult, if not impossible. Present your client's case in a polite, calm, reasoned way. Avoid argument and manner of presentation more suitable for a jury trial where victory, not compromise, is the goal. Save the "make war not peace" approach for trial if the case does not settle.

STAGE ONE: PRE-MEDIATION ADVOCACY.

I am a firm believer in pre-mediation advocacy; by that I mean educating your mediator and your opponent prior to the mediation. The goal is to make certain that they appreciate the important facts and applicable law to ensure a proper evaluation of the case. Although this aspect has been discussed in detail in Chapters 11 and 12, a bit of repetition is warranted.

Pre-mediation advocacy may involve joint conference calls with the mediator and opposing counsel to inform the mediator as to the type of case and the principal issues. It may also involve individual private telephone discussions with the mediator to discuss your side of the case – pre-mediation private caucuses, in effect.

Pre-mediation advocacy involves the submission of written materials. You may wish to provide these to both the mediator and opposing counsel or only to the mediator. Many mediators ask for such submissions, but even if they do not make such a request, you should provide one.

They need not be formal – emails, letters or memoranda may suffice. Include a brief factual summary and why you believe your client is likely to prevail at trial. Where appropriate, depending upon the nature and complexity of the case, support your opinion with excerpts of case law, statutes, key documents and depositions, as well as witness statements, affidavits, photographs, diagrams, charts, customary jury instructions or anything else you believe will strengthen your case. Highlight portions you rely on. These provide you the opportunity to frame the issues and enable the mediator to think in advance about what you believe is important.

STAGE TWO: AT THE BEGINNING – THE JOINT SESSION.

It is a given that good advocacy begins with good preparation. Not only do you want to convince the mediator that you are ready, willing and able to present an effective case at trial, but it is even more important to convince your opponent of that. Be prepared – and look the part.

Remember that when you present your clients' cases at mediation you are not required to convince opponents that you are right and they are wrong. After all, do you believe they will convince you that they are right and you are wrong? Not very often. The other side does not need to agree with you but, rather, needs to be persuaded that a settlement should be reached because of the uncertainty and risks of going to trial.

What is your most important weapon at mediation? I believe it is doubt. You need to create doubt that engenders a fear of losing at trial. Why do cases settle? Because clients and lawyers recognize that there is a risk of losing.

In the joint session, make a presentation that lays the ground work for the negotiations that will follow. Come across as credible, prepared, and knowledgeable. Don't make a jury argument. Don't make an appellate argument. Make an "I would like to reach a reasonable settlement today" argument.

Avoid grandstanding for your client. Such posturing is always counter-productive. Don't insult the other side and avoid statements that will make the other side angry. Take, for example, what might be said in a product liability case. It is not likely to be helpful for the plaintiff's counsel to say in a strongly accusatory tone, "Acme Industries, Inc., intentionally hid product design defects solely to make money out of greed and clearly didn't care about how many people it maimed or killed." It is more likely to be helpful to say in a calm, firm and reasoned manner, "Based upon all the evidence gathered in discovery, including the testimony of your client's own engineers and marketing people, a jury could easily decide that Acme's main concern was making money and not the safety and well being of those who used its product." The message is the same but its wording reduces the likelihood of a harmful emotional reaction. Set the stage for a successful result by creating doubt and fear about what a jury might do, not by creating hostility.

Similarly, it doesn't help for defense counsel to say, "Your client was foolish, irresponsible, didn't know what he was doing in using our product and is lying about how badly he was hurt and how this has affected his life." Instead, saying, "Based on the evidence gathered in discovery, including your client's own testimony and the doctors who treated him, a jury could easily decide that he didn't use Acme's product correctly and he isn't hurt as badly as he believes he is." The message is the same and reduces the likelihood of a plaintiff's emotional, angry reaction.

In opening sessions, avoid addressing one's remarks to the mediator as one would when arguing a motion to a judge; remember that the mediator is not the decision maker. The decision maker is sitting across the table from you. Be sure to speak directly to that decision maker. This does not mean you should exclude the mediator, however. There will be times when you will want to look directly at the mediator and emphasize certain points.

Visual material is important. What is seen makes a greater impact than what is heard. When appropriate, use demonstrative aids such as charts, diagrams, old fashioned blow-ups of documents, deposition testimony, photographs, a video of a scene, portions of video depositions, video of witness statements and PowerPoint presentations. You may even want to bring in fact or expert witnesses, or, you may want them to be available by telephone in order to conference them in.

Your client is also an important part of your advocacy even if he or she does not speak. "Visual advocacy" includes your client's appearance and behavior. You want the other side to believe a jury will like your client because, if the jury does, chances for your success at trial may be increased.

There is no hard and fast rule as to whether a client should speak, but there are times lawyers are opposed to their client's saying anything. They fear that the client may say something harmful, a risk they don't want to take. If your client is going to speak, however, you must prepare him or her thoroughly.

STAGE THREE: DURING THE MEDIATION – PRIVATE CAUCUSES.

Following the opening joint session, a third form of advocacy takes place in the private caucuses. Here you will discuss the issues and the evidence that supports your case and the reasons why you believe a jury will decide in your favor. Be prepared to review and answer questions about your joint session presentation as well as that of your opponent. Emphasize what you believe is important for your mediator to discuss with the other side. Always remember that your goal is to create doubt in your opponent's mind. One of the ways to accomplish this is by making sure the mediator discusses with your opponent what you have emphasized as the strengths of your case and the weaknesses of its side.

What is one of your goals in the private caucuses? Frankly, it is to spin the mediator. Mediators know that lawyers posture and will likely make assertions about liability and damages they really don't believe. That is part of the normal advocacy process. However, the mediator can't be sure what and how much you really believe, or what and how much you don't. If you can persuade the mediator that you truly believe what you say, that message will be conveyed to the other side.

You will want to convince the mediator that you are confident and not afraid to try the case, but be careful not to exaggerate. You want your mediator to find what you say credible so it will be used, and not ignored, when your mediator is talking to the other side.

As the mediation progresses, typically you will move toward a blend of advocacy and good old fashioned negotiation. With a mediator you have confidence in, you may find it helpful to become more candid and discuss concerns you have about your client's case. This conversation gains importance when you need the mediator to help you with a client who is not being realistic. You may also make suggestions to the mediator for getting the case resolved. Don't hesitate to do this – mediators appreciate your help.

Don't be afraid to ask the mediator about his or her thoughts. Your mediator is aware of what is going on in the other room and, without violating any confidences, may provide some helpful guidance as to what approaches could be constructive as negotiations progress.

It is not unusual for a question to arise as to whether or not certain aspects of the case should be kept confidential. Disclosure is often helpful. If you are close to settlement, but not quite there, disclosure of something you have been holding back may move the other side to where you need it to reach a settlement.

STAGE FOUR: NEAR THE END-IMPASSE?

You have reached the point where your patience has run out. You believe a settlement cannot be reached. What type of advocacy may help before you and your client depart? Frequently, when the personal relations between counsel have been good, one of the most effective approaches is to meet with your opposing counsel with or without the mediator. Although threatening to walk out is not usually effective advocacy, looking your opposing counsel in the eye and telling him or her that they just aren't where they need to be, and that you are ready to end the mediation, may result in candid discussions that break the log-jam. You probably don't need to reargue the facts and the law extensively. Instead, impress upon your opponent that your belief in your case is strong and sincere and that you are not posturing (even though you may be to some extent).

Another approach is to tell the mediator, in a calm way, that you believe it is time to end the mediation, and let the mediator communicate this to the other side. This declaration can sometimes produce a positive result as it provides the mediator the opportunity to test the other side by asking, "Do you really want them to leave and end it?" Or, "I am not telling you who is right and who is wrong, but if you really want to settle the case I think you need to ...." Or, "I am not telling you what the case is worth, but to settle it today you will have to be in the range of $_____ to $_____." These remarks often constitute a reality check for the other side.

Don't be passive and wait for the mediator to do it all. Make suggestions for what you think the mediator should do. That is important mediation advocacy.

STAGE FIVE: POST-MEDIATION ADVOCACY.

Your mediation has ended without a settlement being reached. Is this the end of your advocacy? No.

Ask your mediator to remain engaged. Tell your mediator you would like follow-up private telephone calls to be made. Post-mediation advocacy involves keeping your mediator working. Doing so will often lead to a settlement being reached.

Chapter 15

NEGOTIATION AT MEDIATION

"Success – it is what you do with what you got."

WOODY HAYES

At its heart mediation is assisted negotiation. Your mediator, although impartial, is your "assistor."

Mediation negotiations should actually begin before you ever walk in the door. If you follow the steps recommended in Chapter 13, "Prepare Your Opponent for Mediation," you will have taken this important step. Make certain that your opponent has the necessary information to evaluate your client's strengths, his or her client's weaknesses, and the uncertainty and risk faced at trial if the case is not settled.

At the same time, as you begin to negotiate, it is important to realistically assess your client's case. Beyond the posturing that is always part of the negotiation process, what are its true strengths and weaknesses? What are the strengths and weaknesses of your opponent's case? Think through what you believe could be your best, worst and most likely result at trial if the case is not settled.

At the mediation, negotiations don't begin with the first private caucuses and exchange of numbers. They actually begin with the presentations at the joint session. At the joint session it is important to appear confident, well prepared and organized. By focusing on the strengths of your client's case, and the weaknesses of your opponent's, you are staking out your position and setting the stage for the exchange of numbers which will follow.

Once again, I believe doubt is your most important weapon at mediation. Creating it is a prime negotiating technique. Doubt results in concerns about risk, and concerns about risk create fear of losing. Fear of losing moves a party towards a result you want to achieve.

As you negotiate, continue to avoid creating a rancorous atmosphere. Anger just gets in the way of your goal to settle the case. Why make that more difficult than it should be? If you represent the plaintiff, why would you needlessly antagonize the one you want to pay your client money? If you represent the defendant, why would you needlessly antagonize the one you want to accept the best offer you are willing to make? Effective negotiations require setting and maintaining the right tone.

Although negotiations always begin by plaintiffs asking for more than they expect to get and defendants offering less than they are willing to pay, it is important to avoid insulting demands or offers. Such unrealistic posturing inevitably delays the process of getting to what will really settle the case. "Posturing" and "puffing" are an expected part of the process, but overdoing it in an unrealistic way will be destructive to the ongoing negotiations.

At the beginning it is normal for each side to test the other with meaningless numbers. As the private caucuses and negotiations continue, movement toward a successful end result must involve more realistic figures.

Keep an open mind. Go into the mediation with a target, but be flexible. In every negotiation each side typically has two numbers. For the plaintiff, they are what is wanted and what will be accepted. For the defendant, they are what is wanted to be paid and what will be paid. Most successful negotiations arrive at a "willing," not a "wanted," number for both sides.

Negotiations typically involve incremental steps as demand, offers, counter-demands and counter-offers continue to be exchanged. Be patient while they occur. These steps send messages. Beware the "3 O'Clock Syndrome" (although the exact hour may actually vary). I call it the "3 O'Clock Syndrome" based upon my experiences in representing clients in mediations, as well as in serving as a mediator. In most serious cases there would come a time, often around 3:00 PM, when one or both sides would become frustrated and think there was no possibility that a settlement could be reached. However, if the mediator encourages continuing negotiations, more often than not, success would be achieved within an hour or two.

It is important to listen to your mediator. He or she is the only one who knows what is going on in each room. While you negotiate, use your mediator's insights as you work toward reaching your final settlement position.

It is also important not to give a bottom line too soon. Rushing the process is not helpful. A key to successful negotiation is to keep talking as each side becomes more realistic in its expectations. Remember that threatening to walk out is seldom a useful negotiation technique. If you make that threat, be prepared to follow through. I have mediated cases where that threat was made but not carried out, resulting in a loss of credibility and an appearance of weakness. It doesn't help get you to where you want to be.

And don't forget one-on-one meetings of the lawyers involved. Just as they can have an important role in advocacy, the same is true for negotiations.

Lastly, always remember something said by an anonymous mediator:

"You've got to hang the meat low enough to get the dog to jump for it."

Chapter 16

MULTI-PARTY MEDIATIONS

"If everyone is moving forward together,
then success takes care of itself."

Multi-party mediations can be particularly troublesome for both lawyers and mediators. They may present both practical difficulties as well as ethical concerns, and the classic "like herding cats" simile is commonly appropriate.

What practical difficulties frequently arise for defendants? In cases involving money, each defendant has the same interest – paying as little as possible. This focus frequently results in finger pointing on liability and damages. Where liability issues exist there will be arguments about who bears the greater responsibility for injuries suffered. Where only damages issues exist there will be arguments about who should pay what amount into a common fund necessary to settle the case. And, of course, it is not unusual for both of these to be points of contention.

Where there are disagreements over degrees of liability and responsibility for damages, it may be best to have two mediations. During the first, involving only the defendants, the liability and responsibility for damages issues will be negotiated. Once an agreement is reached on these issues, mediating with the plaintiff will occur.

In mediating degrees of fault and responsibility for damages between or among defendants, one approach is to prepare a "ballot" which is provided to each defendant. They may take different forms but one which some mediators use has three columns. The first column will list each defendant. The second is headed "Percentage of Fault" and the third, "Appropriate Contribution." On its ballot, each defendant will write down what percentage of fault and amount of contribution it is believed each defendant should bear for a global settlement. The defendants do not consult one another during the balloting.

The ballots are then given to the mediator and the mediator prepares a summary of the results for the defendants. Copies of the ballot, kept anonymous, may or may not be provided to them. In some cases, multiple ballots will be used as negotiations continue.

An advantage of this exercise is that it gives the defendants important information on what must be negotiated between or among them; it reveals individual positions on major versus minor players and "equality" of defendants. It may also help provide a "reality check" to a defendant who is not being realistic as to responsibility and risk assessment when confronted with what the other defendants believe.

A goal for defendants is to create a common fund that will result in a global offer being made to the plaintiff(s). Ultimately, each defendant needs to focus on individual risk assessment and avoid getting hung up on what percentage he/she/it will contribute. Of course, if the goal of creating a common fund cannot be achieved, defendants may decide to negotiate separate settlements. Informing a recalcitrant defendant of the intent to do this will often result in a decision to "get back in the game."

Lawyers who represent multiple plaintiffs often face some difficult issues, one of which may be equitable division of settlement funds. When their clients cannot agree on such division, ethical problems in the form of conflict of interest result. Also, what happens when one client wants to settle and the other does not and there are limited settlement funds? What about a situation where one client wants to settle, but another does not, and the opposing party will only settle if both clients agree to? Or, what happens when both clients want to settle with limited settlement resources and they want their lawyer to do the apportioning? Or, where a defendant requires that all claims be settled for an aggregate amount, leaving it to the plaintiffs to apportion the settlement fund, and they want their lawyer to decide the amounts?

When one client wants to settle and another does not, it may be necessary to withdraw and advise that each retain new, separate counsel to deal solely with the settlement issue. Or, at minimum, obtain permission from the non-settling client to participate in settling the other's claim. If this route is followed, full disclosure must be made, and informed consent must be obtained, after explanation of the possible adverse consequences, in order to protect yourself from against possible allegations of malpractice or unethical conduct.

When there are limited resources, it is best not to be involved in an apportionment. Ideally, the clients can reach an agreement on this, or if they can't, they should be encouraged to retain separate counsel to negotiate an apportionment, perhaps through additional mediation or even arbitration.

Where there is an aggregate offer for settlement of multiple claims, clients should be fully advised on the significance of the offer and give informed consent to the decision to settle if that is what they want to do. But here again, as with the limited resources situation, advise them to obtain separate counsel to assist them if they can't reach an agreement on the division.

What if prior to a mediation it is learned, or believed, that the clients will either take divergent positions at the mediation or that they may do so? For the "will" scenario, it would be appropriate to persuade the clients to agree to associate separate counsel for the purposes of the mediation. For the "may" scenario, a determination of the need to withdraw could be reserved until it is clear whether or not resolution satisfactory to each client is achievable. But here again, informed consent of the clients is required; withdrawal, and obtaining separate counsel for the mediation may ultimately be necessary.

In cases where different counsel represent separate plaintiffs, difficulties arise when there is a limited amount of money available to settle their cases. As with the multiple defendants situation, a ballot approach might be used to obtain views on who should receive what percentage of the offer that is on the table; and this information may be then used as a starting point for discussions that can result in agreement on apportionment.

It should be expected that where there are multiple defendants or multiple plaintiffs represented by different lawyers, initial agreement as to who pays what, or who gets paid what may be very unlikely. And it should also be anticipated that in cases where multiple plaintiffs or defendants are represented by the same lawyer, ethical problems may arise.

Chapter 17

MEDIATING BUSINESS DISPUTES

*"The fire you kindle for your enemy often
burns yourself more than him."*

CHINESE PROVERB

For the sake of simplicity, much of this book presents discussions assuming that money is the sole concern in settling a case, but business disputes frequently involve more than money. Although the fundamentals of the mediation process, preparation, advocacy and negotiation, still apply, counseling business clients on the reasons to mediate, and the advantages of mediation, is quite often different.

When counseling clients involved in business disputes, either prior to or after the commencement of litigation, what should be discussed to help them understand why mediation makes business sense? Obviously, advising them on the disadvantages of going to court and the advantages of not doing so is important. Additionally, taking them through a cost-benefit analysis can drive these points home.

What disadvantages of litigation, and advantages of mediation, should be discussed? The following are among the most significant:

1. Cost. Business people are concerned about how expensive litigation is. In some cases it may be possible to resolve a dispute for less than the ultimate legal costs of going to trial, not to mention those with a possible appeal. Explaining that the vast majority of cases settle at some point without going to trial, and that mediating their dispute sooner rather than later can result in significant savings, will be important to them.

2. Disruption of Focus on Business. Litigation results in personnel spending unproductive amounts of time away from day-to-day business activities. This scenario is particularly harmful in a significant dispute where management and other key personnel must devote time and attention to it. Resolving a dispute through mediation allows them to focus on what makes their business money instead of spending money on on-going litigation.

3. Lack of Control Over a Final Result. Outcomes of lawsuits where jury trials are involved are unpredictable. Mediation eliminates this risk by allowing clients, not strangers in a jury box, to control the outcome of their dispute.

4. Time. Litigation often goes on for a substantial period of time, frequently a number of years, increasing both cost and a potential disruption of business focus. And what if there is an appeal?

5. Lack of Confidentiality. A trial is a public proceeding. Exposing a business' "dirty laundry" or information it does not want business rivals or competitors, or those it does business with to know about, may be inevitable. Mediation can help protect a business' reputation, confidential information, and trade secrets.

6. Damage to Important Business Relationships. Litigation with a company or individual that is important to a business may result in more harm than benefit, even if there is a victory at trial.

Mediation can assist in the preservation of business relationships that will result in future monetary benefits as terms of a settlement are ironed out.

7. <u>Only One Winner</u>. At a trial one side wins, and the other side loses. The parties give up the opportunity to reach a compromise that is in their mutual best interests. On the other hand, mediation provides flexibility – for example, an agreement to buy or sell future goods or services, or, renegotiating the terms of a contract. Solutions can be tailored beyond only paying out or receiving money.

In addition to discussing the disadvantages of litigation, and the advantages of mediation, assisting a business client in performing a cost-benefit analysis is frequently very helpful. A typical analysis will include the following topics:

1. What is the problem that caused the dispute?
2. What is the history of the business relationship?
3. How does the problem that caused the dispute affect the business?
4. Have there been any discussions with representatives of the adverse party as to possible ways to resolve the dispute?
5. What are the advantages of settling?
6. What are the possible adverse consequences of not settling?
7. What is the financial risk involved?
8. For a plaintiff: How much are you likely to recover after fees and expenses and how does that relate to a potential settlement amount?
9. For a defendant: How much are you likely to spend in fees and expenses and how does that relate to a potential settlement amount?

10. Based on the advantages of settling and risks faced, what are acceptable outcomes in reaching an out-of-court resolution?

Counseling a business client on mediation is important for all disputes likely to lead to, or actually in, litigation. Mediation allows business judgments to be made. Trials do not.

Chapter 18

PSYCHOLOGICAL BARRIERS TO SUCCESS

"The mind is like a parachute – it works only when it is open."

AUTHOR UNKNOWN

O kay – here are some things we learned about when we took Psychology 101 but have probably forgotten over the years. A refresher is important because some of these biases and barriers come up at just about every mediation.

Because lawyers are human (despite what some non-lawyers think), they experience the same psychological reactions as non-lawyers. These instinctive reactions should be recognized by counsel and mediators as potential barriers for success.

Some common psychological barriers include:

* "Advocacy Bias": Self-serving judgments that are believed to be objective but are not because they are based upon one's position in a particular matter, *i.e.*, thinking about strengths without giving sufficient thought to weaknesses.

* "Assimilation Bias": The tendency to see or hear only what one wants to see and hear – that is, information which supports your position.
* "Attributional Bias": The tendency to be hostile to adversaries and impute a negative intent which may not be there.
* "Certainty Bias": Overestimating the degree of certainty in answering questions, assessing a likely result or predicting an outcome.
* "Cognitive Dissonance": The fact that people don't like to consider information that contradicts their viewpoint, resulting in the tendency to deny, downplay or ignore conflicting information.
* "Endowment Effect": Overvaluing the worth of one's claim while undervaluing that of another.
* "Reactive Devaluation": Rejecting proposals by adversaries just because they made them, *i.e.,* "If they want it, I don't."
* "Selective Perception": Overestimating the merits of one's position while underestimating the merits of another's.

Several of these psychological concepts overlap or blend together to create what some have called "Optimism Bias" or "Overconfidence Bias." One of a mediator's most important jobs is to help counsel and parties recognize their biases, or at least move beyond them, as they negotiate and work toward resolving their legal dispute in a way that makes sense.

Chapter 19

WHAT MEDIATORS DO TO HELP SETTLE CASES

*"Patience, persistence and perspiration make
an unbeatable combination for success."*

NAPOLEON HILL

Going into a mediation, it is helpful to think about what mediators are and do. Mediators are neutrals. Their ethical responsibility is to remain impartial. They don't make decisions on who wins and who loses. That is for judges and juries. At the same time, however, they do have "power," the power to help the parties assess their positions more objectively by cutting through posturing, rhetoric and reducing unrealistic expectations.

The fundamental goal of any mediator is to help the parties settle their dispute, and mediators take pride in achieving a successful resolution. Mediators understand that the goals of the parties are never the same. A mediator's job is to assist in working through the changes in positions and goals that are necessary for settlement.

While adhering to the principle of self-determination, that is, that the decision to agree to a settlement is in the hands of the parties alone, mediators can influence the parties as they work to reach a settlement that they, not the mediator, conclude is in their best interests. Mediation is assisted negotiation, and the mediators are the "assistors" in helping the parties reach their decisions.

Mediators use a number of techniques in order to help the parties reach a resolution of their dispute at the different phases of a mediation:

* Pre-mediation
* Initial joint session
* Private caucuses
* Apparent impasse
* Actual impasse/Post-mediation

This discussion of various techniques is meant to be representative, not exhaustive. Mediators may elect not to use some of them because of their training, expertise, philosophies, rules of a jurisdiction or the particular case involved. Mediation is an art, not a science, as is the practice of law.

MEDIATOR TECHNIQUES

PRE-MEDIATION

A mediator wants the parties to consider the details of their case in advance of the mediation. To accomplish this goal many mediators request pre-mediation submissions. As discussed in Chapter 12, these need not be formal but should include a discussion of a party's views of the facts and the law and, where appropriate, copies or excerpts of documents, discovery responses, motions, briefs, depositions, etc. Preparing and providing such submissions not only causes a party's counsel to focus on the case, it helps the mediator know what a case involves, understand a party's positions, and think about what he or she might do during the negotiations to help achieve settlement.

As also discussed in Chapter 12, pre-mediation telephone calls may be useful and sometimes suggested by a mediator. They may be joint, including all counsel, or private, during which individual counsel are asked to talk about a client's side of the case and delineate/outline any special concerns or potential barriers to a settlement.

For those less experienced in mediations, a mediator might provide counsel for the parties written recommendations as to what they can/should do for the mediation. An example is at Appendix C entitled "An ADR Program's Recommendations for a Successful Mediation."

JOINT SESSION

A mediator wants to establish the right tone at the beginning of the mediation, an effort that typically begins during his or her opening remarks. Although counsel, and others experienced in mediations, will have heard similar remarks before, they should bear with the mediator. A mediator wants to establish a comfortable, yet serious, level of informality for the proceedings. More often than not, opening remarks are principally directed toward clients who have little or no experience in mediations. Their purpose is to reduce anxieties, create an understanding of the mediation process and make it easier for clients to deal with the substantive discussions and negotiations which will follow.

In the joint session a mediator wants to begin to establish rapport and build trust with the parties. Additionally, as counsel present their views of the case, a mediator wants to be seen as a good listener who is hearing what a party believes is important.

PRIVATE CAUCUSES

Virtually all mediations include multiple private caucuses and mediators do different things as these continue.

In the initial private caucus, a mediator typically asks some general questions and listens to what the attorney and client want to say, such as:

"Is there anything you want to discuss privately that you didn't want to talk about in the joint session?"

"Tell me what you believe is most important for me to talk to the other side about?" "Why is it?"

"In the opposing attorney's remarks in the joint session he said . . . . Give me your take on that."

"What are the possible barriers to reaching a settlement today?" "Why are they present?"

While asking questions in the initial caucus a mediator will take care not to be perceived as expressing opinions that could result in a questioning of his or her impartiality status. If it is believed that the mediator is taking sides, his effectiveness will, at best, be highly compromised and, more likely, be destroyed.

In the second private caucus, a mediator often begins to engage in "reality testing," a process that will continue through subsequent caucuses. The purpose of reality testing is to deal with "advocacy bias" (believing your case is stronger than it may be), unrealistic expectations and overconfidence as to the outcome of a trial. Such psychological barriers have been discussed in Chapter 18.

Examples of initial reality testing questions are:

"They believe they will be able to . . . ." "What should I tell them in response to that?"

"They believe you won't be able to . . . ." "What should I tell them in response to that?"

"What do you understand their main argument to be?" "Why would they think it is a valid one?"

"They emphasize . . . ." "What should I tell them in response to that?"

Subsequent caucuses questions may include:

"How can this conflicting testimony be explained?"

"What type jury are you likely to get?"

"Do you think a jury will buy that?"

"Do you think a judge is going to let that evidence come in?"

"Do you think you can win on a motion for summary judgment?" "What about a motion for directed verdict?"

"What do you believe they think are their strengths?" "Why do you think they believe that?" "Why could they believe that?"

"What do you believe they think are your weaknesses?" "Why do you think they believe that?" "Why could they believe that?"

"What concerns do you have about your side of the case?" "Why?"

To the plaintiff: "What do you think they want to pay?" "Why do you think that?"

To the defendant: "What do you think they want?" "Why do you think that?"

"If you tried this case ten times, how many times would you get a verdict in your favor?"

To the plaintiff: "Assuming you do win, what do you believe the range of the verdict could be (not what it would be)?"

To the defendant: "Assuming you do lose, what do you believe the range of the verdict could be (not what it would be)?"

"If the case were tried ten times, how many times do you think the other side would believe it will win?"

To the plaintiff: "What do you think the defense believes is the highest verdict a jury would award?" "The lowest?" "The most likely?"

To the defendant: "What do you think the plaintiff believes is the lowest verdict a jury would award?" "The highest?" "The most likely?"

To the plaintiff: "What is the most you believe they will pay?" "Why do you believe that?"

To the defendant: "What is the least you believe they will take?" "Why do you believe that?"

"Do you think you could guarantee your client a win if you went to court?"

"If you were to win at trial, do you think the other side is likely to appeal?"

One goal of these type questions is to encourage parties to move away from thinking only about their analysis and evaluation of the case and to get them thinking about that of their opponent. Another goal is that parties will think about the risk of losing and understand that if they lose, they will come out worse than if they had agreed to a settlement at the mediation.

As discussed in Chapter 3, there are two common approaches that mediators use in private caucuses. The first, the "facilitative," is the classic mediation technique that was first developed. In using it, as demonstrated by the open-ended questions above, a mediator does not directly express opinions. The objective is to motivate the parties to think more realistically about their risks and negotiating positions.

Recall that the second approach, "evaluative mediation," is one not all mediators use. Some believe it impinges upon the fundamental principle of self-determination, and some courts prohibit it for the same reason. Or, in areas where it is not prohibited, it may only be used in certain types of cases. In the evaluative approach, opinions are expressed on the case, including such aspects as credibility of witnesses, impact of governing law, what a jury is likely to believe, strengths or weaknesses of the case, possible results of a trial, settlement value, etc.

Although some mediators and courts believe that the facilitative approach is the only proper one, in that it does not affect self-determination, it has become increasingly common for mediators to utilize both facilitation and evaluation as a mediation progresses. They begin with facilitation and later move on to varying degrees of evaluation if they believe sufficient rapport and trust in their impartiality has been established. In fact, mediators are frequently asked by attorneys or parties to express opinions on some aspect of a case. Some surveys and articles indicate that many lawyers want a mediator to express opinions when asked to do so – and, on occasion, even when an opinion has not been requested.

The evaluative technique may begin indirectly, by the way a question is asked, facial expressions, body language, or remarks such as, "If I had your side of the case this is what would concern me . . . ."

Sometimes mediators may offer suggestions for settlement proposals they believe could be helpful, or they may express an opinion on a settlement range to consider. It may be suggested that "brackets" be used when explaining settlement ranges. For example, a plaintiff's proposal stating, "Tell them that I will come down to $100,000 if they will come up to $85,000," or a defendant's proposal stating, "Tell them that I will come up to $50,000 if they come down to $70,000." While almost never accepted, mediators know brackets can send signals as to potential zones for a settlement to be reached, and many mediators encourage their use.

Additional strategies for mediators, whether facilitating or evaluating are:

Expressing optimism in the face of impatience or frustration.

Keeping the parties talking when they begin to express pessimism about reaching a settlement but the mediator believes one still may be possible.

Talking about their experiences, or the experiences of others, that highlight the possible results or uncertainties of litigation and trials.

Encouraging parties to think about the costs which will be incurred if the case doesn't settle.

Helping a lawyer with an unrealistic client.

Helping lawyers and/or clients save face by talking about "new information" or a "new way" to think about the case based upon a development that justifies a change in what was previously said to be a firm position. An example is, "We have gained some new information. Based upon this new information could you consider making a new decision?"

Where more than just money is involved, as in business or domestic cases, a good strategy is to work toward agreements on the easier matters first in order to build momentum.

APPARENT IMPASSE

Okay. None of the things discussed above have resulted in a settlement. It appears that the mediation is about to end. What might a mediator do then?

One technique is to call a meeting of lawyers with the mediator. The mediator says, "I think it could be helpful if you talk face to face and tell the other lawyer why you are where you are." The mediator opens the meeting by talking about what he or she sees as the obstacle(s) to reaching an agreement and asks the lawyers to talk to one another about it/ them. This approach often reduces posturing and creates understanding as to why certain positions are being taken. It is not uncommon for these meetings to be helpful in reaching a successful conclusion.

A mediator may also use the "What if . . . ." technique. "What if I could get them to pay $90,000? Would you consider it?" "What if I could get them to take $80,000? Would you consider it?" Or, it may not be "consider" but, instead, simply "take" and "pay."

A "last best offer," "last best demand" approach may sometimes help. The mediator asks for these and states that they will be kept confidential. If the parties are close to an agreement, the mediator will tell them so and declare that it obviously now makes sense to show a bit more flexibility. He might comment, "You are closer than the cost to litigate and try the case." Or, "I believe you should consider moving a bit more because of the time it will take to get to trial and the elimination of the uncertainties and risks involved." The mediator's goal is to keep parties talking when he or she believes that doing so may be productive.

Sometimes throwing things back on the lawyers is useful: "I have done what I know to do. This is my problem . . . . What can you do to help me?" Or, "What do you recommend I do?"

A mediator may ask the parties to make a conditional offer, as for the defendant, "I will pay $60,000 if you will take it." Or, for the plaintiff, "I will take $75,000 if you will pay it."

Another approach may be for the mediator to make a "mediator's proposal." The mediator privately provides each side with the identical number proposed to be paid and accepted to settle the case. The mediator may say something like, "I am not saying who should win or who should lose. I am not telling you what the case is worth. What I am telling you is what I believe has the potential to settle it." If both say "no," the mediator announces that there is no settlement. If one side says "yes" and the other side says "no," the mediator announces that there is no settlement and does not disclose to the non-accepting party that the other party did accept it. Only if both sides agree to the mediator's number is it announced that the case is settled. This technique, often called the "silver bullet," sometimes succeeds.

When all other approaches fail, there are several approaches a mediator might suggest for consideration by the parties: in business or domestic cases, a partial settlement; in "money only" cases, a High-Low agreement; an agreement to arbitrate using a different neutral.

ACTUAL IMPASSE/POST-MEDIATION

When no approach has worked, the mediator may suggest that the parties agree to adjourn the mediation rather than terminate it. This delay can provide additional time for further discovery and investigation as well as simply the opportunity to think about what led to the impasse. "Adjourning" rather than "terminating" sometimes has psychological benefits, and it is not uncommon for a settlement to occur without the need to reconvene.

Lastly, a conscientious mediator will follow-up with telephone calls to counsel in an effort to keep them talking.

Chapter 20

WHAT LAWYERS LIKE AND "HATE" ABOUT

MEDIATORS AND MEDIATION

"The single most important key to
success is to be a good listener."

KELLY WEARSTLER

Over the years, as I have chaired continuing legal education programs on mediation, I have learned that it always works well to
use a panel, equally divided between plaintiff and defense attorneys, to
discuss what they like and dislike about mediation and mediators.

Here are some typical comments about what lawyers like about
mediation:

* Self-determination, the ability to control one's own destiny is
possible.
* It removes the uncertainty of what will happen at trial.
* It makes the lawyer get prepared.
* It is a much more efficient way to resolve a case. It saves time
and money.

* It lets a client tell his or her story to an "authority figure," not just his or her lawyer. Some clients need to do this.
* It gets lawyers and decision makers for both sides to focus on the case at the same time.
* It educates a client and provides reality checks.
* It involves much less stress and anxiety for clients than going to court (and the same for lawyers as well).
* Complex cases are more likely to settle at mediation than through the traditional negotiation process.
* Confidentiality allows for frank discussions and expression of concerns to the mediator.
* When a lawyer needs help with an unrealistic client, the mediator can provide it.

Here are some typical comments about what lawyers don't like about mediation:

* The other party comes with no intention to settle.
* The other party's main goal is to gain insights into how you will present your case.
* Court-ordered mediation when lawyers for both sides know there is no possibility a case can be settled.
* Court-ordered mediation that is required too soon.
* Unrealistic initial demands and counter-offers which waste time.
* Opposing counsel who are unprepared to negotiate in a meaningful way.
* Adjusters who attend without sufficient settlement authority.

Here are some typical comments on what lawyers like in mediators:

* The ability to develop rapport with clients and gain their trust.
* Talking to the parties and not just the lawyers.
* Persistence.

* Directness with lawyers and clients when necessary.
* The ability to sense when a lawyer needs help with a client.
* The ability to provide meaningful "reality checks."
* Creativity – the ability to avoid the sole role of "numbers messenger."
* Offering opinions at the right time.
* Fostering continuing negotiations when a case does not settle; making follow- up telephone calls to the lawyers.

Here are some typical comments on what lawyers don't like about mediators:

* Not reviewing pre-mediation submissions and not being prepared.
* Not being knowledgeable on the law when it is important in a case.
* Being a passive participant, a messenger who only exchanges numbers.
* Being a poor facilitator.
* Not expressing opinions when they are asked for.
* Moving too fast.
* Giving up too soon.
* Trying to get a party to accept, or pay, "an absurd number" just to get the case settled.
* Making a mediator's proposal (*i.e.*, suggesting a dollar amount) to settle the case too soon.

Chapter 21

WHAT MEDIATORS "HATE" ABOUT LAWYERS

"If I only had a little humility I would be perfect."

TED TURNER

What are some things mediators really "hate" about lawyers? Here goes.

ONE: CHANGE OF PRE-MEDIATION DEMAND/OFFER

A substantial change in a pre-mediation demand or offer at the mediation causes mediators to think to themselves, "Oh no!" These changes extend the mediation longer than necessary at best, or, at worst, result in a breakdown of meaningful negotiations.

Significant changes typically result in immediate frustration, and sometimes anger, in the other side. A typical response is, "They are not here in good faith!" or "We came prepared to negotiate from the number we were given, not this number!"

At this point a mediator talks to the lawyer about the difficulty his party's changes have caused and explains that this approach is not helpful if he or she sincerely desires to settle the case. The mediator must then ask the other party for time to work through this difficulty to determine if negotiations can get back to the pre-mediation number. Unless this extra time is agreed upon, the likelihood of a successful mediation is not great.

If a pre-mediation demand or offer is going to be changed, it should be accompanied by a reasonable explanation of the reasons for the change and provided far enough in advance of the mediation so that the opposing side has time to re-evaluate its settlement position. A "just because" or last minute explanation is not enough.

TWO: SURPRISE, SURPRISE!

Surprising your opponent with significant new information may be fun at trial, but this tactic does not help during mediation. Settlement positions are thought through prior to the mediation, and risk assessment and valuation are based upon information then available.

When new information is presented that results in a settlement not being reached, the mediator may ask the parties to adjourn, not terminate, the mediation to allow for whatever additional work needs to be done for further case evaluation. The mediator hopes this break will result in the case being settled thereafter within a reasonable period of time.

THREE: TRIAL VERSUS MEDIATION ADVOCACY

There is a difference between "trial advocacy" and "mediation advocacy." Trial advocacy is combative whereas mediation advocacy is conciliatory. The mediator's job of helping you achieve the settlement you desire will be much more difficult if a party sets a needlessly aggressive, unpleasant, hostile or self-righteous tone.

FOUR: PREPARATION MISTAKES

Lack of proper preparation, which includes failure to:

1) Prepare yourself;
2) Prepare the mediator;
3) Prepare your client; and
4) Prepare your opponent.

FIVE: FORGETTING SIGMUND FREUD

"Forgetting Sigmund Freud." What does that mean? It means not being aware of aspects of human psychology that come into play in any adversarial matter. Don't fall into the trap of believing you are the only realistic one, and always be aware of "advocacy bias," the natural tendency to overestimate the strengths of your client's case and weaknesses of your opponent's. A corollary is "certainty bias," the notion that a position is absolutely correct or of what an end result will be (*e.g.*, "I will get more than is being offered at trial." "I will pay less as a result of a jury verdict than I would need to pay today to settle the case." "There is no way I will lose at trial.")

SIX: ASKING FOR HELP WITH A CLIENT, THEN UNDERCUTTING IT

It has happened to every mediator. The mediation has gone on for several hours, and frustration is growing. An attorney pulls the mediator aside and says, "I need some help with my client. He is being unrealistic. Please be direct with him in discussing his case and the risks of losing (or paying more or getting less) in our next private caucus."

So the mediator goes into the room, begins to talk about concerns and risks to be considered, but then the lawyer who asked for help undercuts the mediator's efforts by grandstanding in front of the client! I assume this behavior arises because the lawyer does not want to appear weak or to be caving in. On these occasions, the mediator needs to pull the lawyer aside and ask, "What in the world are you doing? I thought you wanted me to help you get your client to be more realistic."

SEVEN: OVERREACTING TO INITIAL DEMANDS OR OFFERS

Face it. In most mediations, the defendant thinks the plaintiff is starting way too high, and the plaintiff thinks the defendant is starting way too low. Overreacting with assertions such as "They are not here in good faith" or "They must not want to settle the case" are not helpful.

Take the first one or two demands and counter-demands, offers and counter-offers, with a grain of salt. In most mediations, these initial forays into negotiation don't matter. Some early posturing is going on. Stay cool, calm and collected. Let the mediator explain to your client that this is a typical situation and does not mean the case cannot be settled. Let the mediator work with your opponent to encourage realistic movements.

EIGHT: IMPATIENCE WITH THE PROCESS

Most mediations last longer than either side would like. Each side wants to "play poker" and not concede anything too soon. Each side wants to meet or exceed its pre-mediation goal. Each fears that moving too fast will result in giving up too much too soon.

At a mediation, it is not uncommon to reach a point where one or both sides want to throw in the towel, believing that the process just isn't going to work. Keep in mind, however, that it is the mediator's job to keep everyone there as long as he or she believes there is a realistic opportunity for a settlement. The mediator is the only one who knows what is going on in each room and, more often than not, will be able to distinguish between apparent impasses and actual impasses. A good mediator will tell you when an actual impasse has been reached, but he will want to keep everyone working when the "impasse" is only an apparent one. Experience shows that there is almost something magical about the mediation process. Be patient.

NINE: COMING IN WITH A NEGATIVE ATTITUDE

Sometimes one or both of the lawyers will come into a mediation with a negative attitude. They believe that the case will never settle and that they are wasting their time. Sometimes this may be true, but often it is not. It is important to allow enough time to find out if the process can lead to an agreement. Every mediator has mediated cases in which one or more of the lawyers said "It is not going to be possible to settle," but a settlement was reached.

TEN: THREATENING TO WALK OUT

There are times when it is appropriate to walk out, but most of the time it is not. Don't threaten to walk out unless you really mean it. If you make the threat and don't follow through, you will appear weak and lose credibility.

I have mediated cases where a lawyer has instructed me to tell his/her opponent that if "x" isn't done they are going to walk out. I always ask, "Please don't insist I do that. Instead, let me tell them that it appears you may be on the verge of walking out. Let me see what reaction I get." My request is usually granted, but this has not always been the case.

In one case I was instructed three times in succession to tell a defendant's counsel that if the defendant did not come up to "x," then "y," then "z," plaintiff's counsel and client were going to walk out. Neither "x," "y" or "z" was ever the defendant's response, yet none of plaintiff's counsel's successive threats were carried out. The plaintiff's counsel and client did not leave. What impact do you think this had on credibility? On getting to what would really settle the case? On the case being settled?

ELEVEN: NOT SHIFTING FROM ADVOCATE TO COUNSELOR

Mediations begin with the lawyers acting as strong advocates for their clients, the necessary and proper role. They wouldn't be doing their jobs otherwise. The advocate role continues through one or more of the initial caucuses, but at some point in a mediation, the role should shift from advocate to counselor. It is in the counselor role that the lawyer helps clients reach an end result that is in their best interests, even if they don't get exactly what they want. A time often comes when a lawyer needs to tell clients something they don't want to hear, whether it pertains to risk of losing, case value, or both.

TWELVE: STARTING WITH UNREASONABLE DEMANDS/OFFERS

When a lawyer makes an unreasonable demand or offer, he or she should ask, "If I were representing the other side, how would I react to that?" Doesn't that question answer itself? Then why do it?

THIRTEEN: DECISION-MAKER ON THE TELEPHONE

A decision-maker participating by telephone often increases difficulties and delays a settlement. Although you might think a mediator being paid by the hour would appreciate a mediation that lasts longer than necessary, a good mediator does not. His or her job is to help the parties get the case settled, not drag out the process.

FOURTEEN: UNWILLINGNESS TO BE CANDID WITH OR LISTEN TO THE MEDIATOR

You are getting close but are not quite there. At that point, don't fear being candid with your mediator as to what can get the case settled. If your client really wants the case settled, posturing needs to end at some point. Let the mediator know confidentially what will settle the case so he or she can work with your opponent to see if that is achievable.

At the same time, allow the mediator to be candid with you. Listen as he/she talks about concerns he or she would have if representing your client. And, don't be afraid to ask your mediator what he or she thinks. Remember the earlier discussions on advocacy and certainty bias? A neutral mediator is the most objective person involved. Take advantage of that objectivity when a mediator is not prohibited from offering opinions. (See the previous discussions of "evaluative" mediation in Chapters 3 and 19.)

FIFTEEN:"IT'S THE PRINCIPLE!" (NO, IT'S NOT, IT'S THE MONEY!)

How many times have mediators heard someone say, "It's the principle," during a mediation. Nearly every time this "principle" turns out to be money. Pretending that you are standing on principle, when you really are standing on a stack of dollar bills, makes a mediation more difficult and time consuming.

Mediators don't really "hate" lawyers. After all, many are also lawyers, but mediators sometimes get frustrated by them. The mediator's role is to help the lawyers and clients bring a case to an end in a way that they, not the mediator, believe makes sense. Do your best to avoid actions that decrease the opportunity for a successful resolution.

Chapter 22

MEDIATION ETHICS FOR LAWYERS

(YES, THERE ARE SOME!)

"Be influenced by nothing but your clients'
interests. Tell them the truth."

ARTHUR C. NIELSEN

Although it may not be much thought about, ethical rules or considerations do come into play for lawyers at a mediation. These include:

* A duty to advise a client on alternatives to litigation and/or trials.
* Competency and competent representation.
* Avoiding conflict of interest.
* Good faith.
* Proper advocacy and negotiation.
* Maintaining confidentiality.

Both state and federal courts commonly require or encourage mediation, and some require that counsel advise clients on mediation and explain its benefits. Even where it is not required, however, mediation is now a commonly accepted step in the litigation process. Where mediation is not required, might it be concluded that a lawyer has a duty to advise a client on the availability and advantages of mediation as a way to resolve his or her case? What if a lawyer does not give such advice, the case goes to trial, and is lost? Could the lawyer be sued for malpractice for not advising on the availability of, or encouraging, mediation? Could the client take the position that since a very high percentage of cases settle at mediation, the opportunity to achieve a reasonable settlement was lost? Might the client's lawyer attempt to prove through expert testimony that, by a preponderance of the evidence, being able to reach a settlement was more probable than not? And, with perhaps a likely amount? A duty to advise clients on mediation raises not only ethical obligations but also potential malpractice concerns.

COMPETENCY AND COMPETENT REPRESENTATION

A lawyer should be competent in the area of law involved in the mediation. No surprise there.

Competent representation also includes adequate preparation for a mediation. Failure to properly prepare for mediation may be criticized by a client just as a failure to properly prepare for trial may be. Beware of simply "winging it" at mediation.

Competent representation involves discussing the case with a client and informing the client of the case's strengths and weaknesses. Additionally, the following elements should be discussed:

* Benefits and risks of a trial.
* Costs of further litigation and a trial.
* Risks of an appeal.
* Confidentiality of the mediation process.
* Benefits of mediation relating to control of the outcome and certainty of the final result.

* The time in which a matter may be concluded at mediation versus trial.

Competent representation entails preparing the client for the mediation. He or she should be told about what mediation is, who will be involved, the role of the mediator, and the typical mediation process. A client should also be prepared on what to say, or not to say, in both joint and private meetings.

CONFLICT OF INTEREST

Conflict of interest situations in mediations may arise when a lawyer represents multiple parties in the same lawsuit or dispute. What happens when one client wants to settle and the other does not, yet the opposing party will only settle if both clients agree? What happens when both clients want to settle but there are limited settlement resources to be apportioned? Or, when a defendant requires that all claims must be settled for an aggregate amount, leaving it to the parties to apportion the settlement fund? Refer back to the more detailed discussions on the ethical concerns for these situations and others in Chapter 16. Always remember, the safest course will be to withdraw from these settlement aspects of a case so that the settlement issues can be dealt with by separately retained counsel. If you don't withdraw from such settlement aspects, always make certain you provide clients with sufficient information for them to make an informed consent for you to continue handling settlement negotiations should they not wish to retain separate counsel for that purpose.

GOOD FAITH/FULL AUTHORITY TO SETTLE

What does it mean that a party must participate in "good faith?" What does it mean that a party must have someone present at the mediation with "full authority to settle?"

Court ordered mediation will typically require that the parties participate in good faith. Simply put, this means that a party must attend with the intent to engage in good faith negotiations subject to the party's evaluation of the case. Going through the motions to use mediation as a discovery mechanism is not "good faith." However, "good faith" does not require that a party settle. In voluntary (*i.e.*, non-court ordered) mediations, there is an implicit obligation to negotiate in good faith. It is not unusual for a mediator to ask counsel and the parties to sign an "Agreement to Mediate" form which contains a representation that they will negotiate in good faith.

Court ordered mediation typically imposes a requirement that the parties have someone in attendance who can actually agree to a settlement then and there, *i.e.*, who has "full authority to settle." This does not preclude the possibility of the need "to make a call" to a superior to get more settlement authority, not an unusual scenario, particularly when an insurance carrier is involved. It does mean that if a settlement amount and all other necessary terms are agreed to by one party, the other party has the ability to commit to a settlement then and there without the need for its attendee go back to his or her office and run the proposed terms by a superior who has the only authority to commit. In other words, a party must have someone present who has authority to "sign on the dotted line" of a mediation settlement memorandum if an agreement is reached, even when more formal settlement documents are to be executed later.

EX PARTE COMMUNICATIONS

Some courts may decide to prohibit ex parte communications between the mediator and counsel for the parties. Other courts either may permit them or not address them at all.

In private mediations it may not be unusual for counsel for the parties or the mediator to suggest pre-mediation private discussions by telephone. These discussions can address specific areas of concern, *e.g.*, the need for help in getting a client to be realistic, problems with counsel on the other side, perceived barriers to settlement, etc. In effect, these are pre-mediation private caucuses.

Mediators frequently invite confidential written submissions based upon a belief that having information about the case, and the parties' positions, in advance will help expedite the mediation process. It is widely accepted that such submissions do not constitute improper ex parte communications.

Mediation advocacy and negotiation are discussed in Chapters 14 and 15. As pointed out, previously posturing or "puffing" is not unethical. Also, it is accepted that stating opinions as to the value of a claim, which may be either higher or lower than privately believed, is not improper. Nor are statements as to settlement positions which are not truly final ones. Such behavior is regarded as "puffing" or posturing and is permissible.

The American Bar Association Standing Committee on Ethics and Professional Responsibility rendered Formal Opinion 06-439 in 2006 which took the position that posturing and puffing are not unethical and that statements of negotiating goals or willingness to compromise are not false statements of material fact. As the opinion states:

> It is not unusual in negotiation for a party, directly or through counsel, to make a statement in the course of communicating its position **that is less than entirely forthcoming**. (Emphasis added).

For both factual and legal positions, it is permissible to exaggerate or emphasize the strengths and minimize or de-emphasize the weaknesses, of a case.

But what is not permissible? Examples include:

*   Representing that there are documents supporting a client's case that don't exist.

*   Representing that there are witnesses supporting a client's case that don't exist.
*   Misrepresenting what a witness observed or will say.
*   Concealing the death of a client when the death would have a substantive impact on negotiations and the settlement position of an opponent.
*   Stating that the board of directors of a client had formally disapproved any settlement in excess of a stated amount when authority had been granted to settle for a higher sum.

It has been observed that in mediation consensual deception is intrinsic to the process. Such "consensual deception," *i.e.*, negotiation tactic, is not unethical.

CONFIDENTIALITY

The general rule is that what occurs at mediation is to be held confidential. Counsel communicating to the court what the other party or its counsel said or did with respect to substantive matters at the mediation is, without consent, improper. Doing so can result in a motion for sanctions. It is not improper, however, for counsel to advise the court that a mediation occurred, that there was or was not a settlement and, absent a confidentiality agreement, the terms and amount of the settlement. The same limitations apply to communications with third persons who are not parties in the litigation.

Chapter 23

MEDIATION ETHICS FOR MEDIATORS

"The cold neutrality of an impartial judge."

Edmund Burke

Just as counsel for the parties have ethical obligations at mediations, so do mediators. The role of the mediator is to assist in communications and negotiations between the parties, not be a fact finder or decision maker.

Commonly accepted ethical standards for mediators include:

*   Assuring self-determination
*   Assuring voluntariness
*   Maintaining impartiality/neutrality
*   Avoiding conflicts of interest
*   Assuring the integrity of the process
*   Not providing legal or financial advice
*   Maintaining confidentiality
*   Competency to mediate the dispute
*   Truth in advertising and marketing

SELF-DETERMINATION AND VOLUNTARINESS

Self-determination means that the parties make their own decisions. The parties are to make voluntary, not coerced decisions. Their decisions include selection of the mediator, the decision as to continuing or ending the mediation, and the freedom to agree or not agree to a settlement (even if the mediation is required by the Court). A mediator's desire to keep settlement rates high, or impress judges or program directors, should not result in applying improper pressure to settle the case.

IMPARTIALITY/NEUTRALITY

To remain impartial and neutral is central to a mediator's role. A mediator must control his or her feelings or beliefs as to who is in the right and should "win" or who may be wrong and should "lose." A mediator must avoid taking sides, either directly or indirectly. Unlike a neutral arbitrator, the mediator must not act as a fact finder or decision maker as much as he or she may be tempted to take on that role.

AVOIDING CONFLICTS OF INTEREST

Just as lawyers taking on the representation of a client are ethically bound to avoid actual or apparent conflicts of interest, mediators must do the same when they assume the role of mediator. This obligation exists not only with respect to taking on and conducting the mediation but after the mediation has ended as well.

Obviously, where there is a direct interest in the outcome, a mediator must never take on the dispute. Where a potential or indirect conflict of interest is a possibility a mediator should disclose this as soon as it is reasonably known. If after such disclosure, however, the parties agree, it is acceptable for a mediator to continue in the role.

Following a mediation, the mediator must take care to avoid the appearance of a conflict of interest. Taking on a post-mediation professional or personal relationship with a party, whether an individual, company or organization, must be avoided if a perceived or actual conflict of interest could result.

ASSURING THE INTEGRITY OF THE PROCESS

What does assuring the integrity of the process mean? If a mediator learns a party is engaging in a misrepresentation, withdrawal and termination may be required if it is believed that such misrepresentation will, or is likely to affect a party's settlement decision. Similarly, if there is a "power imbalance" between parties, and it is apparent a party is going to be unfairly taken advantage of, withdrawal and termination of the mediation is appropriate. A mediator should not participate in concluding a patently unfair or unconscionable agreement. When a party engages in abusive behavior, threats, or it appears that a party is under the influence of drugs, alcohol or lacking in mental capacity, the mediator should withdraw and terminate the mediation.

The guiding principle of mediation is that a party must be able to freely and willingly enter into an informed agreement. Where such ability is lacking, a mediation should not be allowed to continue.

NOT PROVIDING LEGAL OR FINANCIAL ADVICE

A mediator does not represent a client in a mediation. Although mediators may discuss legal issues, possible results at trial, or financial aspects of a case, they must not provide legal or financial advice. That aspect is left to counsel. Providing such advice is improper and may have malpractice implications for the mediator.

MAINTAINING CONFIDENTIALITY

It has long been the rule that, with limited exceptions, what a mediator learns or is told is confidential and may not be disclosed; this knowledge is not subject to discovery, nor may it be used in any subsequent administrative or judicial proceeding. What occurs during the media-tion process should not be disclosed by the mediator to the Court or third parties. Nor may the mediator disclose to an opposing party what the other party states is confidential, even if the mediator believes that such disclosure would increase the likelihood of a settlement. Continuing to seek permission to disclose is permissible, however.

Common limited exceptions to confidentiality includes:

* Threats of imminent violence to self or others.
* Danger to the safety of a party or third parties.
* Child abuse.
* Whether the parties appeared as ordered.
* Whether settlement occurred and its terms if required for an order of the Court.

COMPETENCY TO MEDIATE THE DISPUTE

Competency for a mediator means that he should not mediate a case for which he is unqualified or lacks the ability to undertake. Taking on a mediation creates an expectation that the mediator's qualifications and abilities are sufficient for assisting in meaningful communications and negotiations between the parties. When a specific expertise is im-portant - for example in a complex patent dispute involving technical issues, only a mediator experienced in that area of the law should serve as mediator.

TRUTH IN ADVERTISING AND MARKETING

Closely allied with competency is truth in advertising and marketing. A mediator is obligated not to mislead as to qualifications and experience. Also important is that promises as to outcome not be made, *i.e.*, that settlement is guaranteed.

RAYMOND G. CHADWICK JD

MEDIATION IS NOT THE PRACTICE OF LAW

The question of whether or not mediation constitutes the unauthorized practice of law has arisen in the past. In most states, the answer is that it does not. The generally held view is that the practice of law must involve an attorney-client relationship and that such relationship does not exist between a party and a mediator. In a mediation, parties do not rely on the mediator to represent their interests. Rather, the mediator is a neutral assisting in settlement discussions and negotiations. The American Bar Association Section on Dispute Resolution has adopted a resolution stating that discussions with the parties of legal issues does not create an attorney-client relationship and does not constitute providing legal advice.

Chapters 3 and 19 discuss evaluative mediation and the limitations some courts place upon it. However, many mediators believe that discussing strengths and weaknesses of a party's case, possible outcomes, a jury's potential reaction to certain facts or arguments, or settlement approaches is permissible in mediations. The generally held view is that doing so does not constitute the practice of law. As discussed earlier, it is not uncommon for attorneys in mediations to ask a mediator in whom they have confidence to express opinions, that is "evaluate," in addition to facilitating discussions and negotiations. And although some courts prohibit evaluative mediation, and some mediators believe the facilitative approach is the only one appropriate for avoiding interference with self-determination, the trend seems to favor allowing evaluative mediation to be utilized by mediators who do not view it as impinging on self-determination. Indeed, those mediators believe evaluation actually assists self-determination as parties more realistically evaluate a case and they, not the mediator, make the final decisions on what they conclude is in their best interests.

Chapter 24

MED-ARB/ARB-MED

"Conflict is inevitable, but combat optional."

MAX LUCADO

"Med-Arb" and "Arb-Med" are terms for hybrids of mediation and arbitration. They are most commonly used in commercial cases when a contract between the parties contains a clause requiring their use if a dispute arises. Sometimes, however, parties agree to one or the other even when not required.

In Med-Arb the first step is mediation. If it does not result in a resolution of the dispute, the parties then arbitrate and are bound by the decision, called an "award," which is rendered by the arbitrator(s).

Why would parties agree to Med-Arb? They believe a resolution will occur more quickly and cost less than engaging in litigation. They also may believe a settlement will be more likely because the parties know they will control the outcome if the mediation is successful, thus avoiding the risk of a binding adverse decision by an arbitrator.

If the mediator is also to be the arbitrator, however, certain concerns arise. During a mediation, confidential discussions and information are shared about a party's concerns, and their perceived strengths and weaknesses, as well as settlement positions. The mediator may discuss his or her evaluation of the case. As an arbitrator, the former mediator is supposed to set these discussions aside and consider only the evidence and governing law. But how does the mediator, now arbitrator, "unring the bell?" Might it not be difficult to ignore what was learned at the mediation?

If Med-Arb is to be used, the best way to avoid the possibility of a "tainted" arbitrator is to choose a different person for the mediator role. If I were to agree to Med-Arb, that is what I would prefer.

The Arb-Med process is designed to avoid the possibility of a "tainted" arbitrator since arbitration comes first. After hearing the case, and considering the evidence and the law, the arbitrator prepares a written decision but does not provide it to the parties. Instead, the arbitrator then moves into the role of mediator.

A major concern of Arb-Med is cost since arbitration can be expensive, certainly more costly than mediation. Although not as formal as a trial, a hearing with presentations of evidence and legal arguments in both oral and written form is required. The arbitrator must take enough time to hear and consider the evidence, review the law and then prepare a written decision that may just be thrown away. A second concern is the question of impartiality. Fundamental to mediation, and an ethical requirement is that mediators must remain impartial as they assist the parties in discussions and negotiations. Will it be difficult for the former arbitrator, now mediator, to maintain impartiality after deciding who should win and who should lose? Or, if the parties request holding the award in abeyance so they can mediate before it is announced, might the now mediator, even unintentionally, signal which side will win and which will lose, thereby affecting a party's decisions?

In Arb-Med, as in Med-Arb, the parties may decide to use a separate arbitrator and mediator. Although it is not uncommon in Arb-Med for the parties to use the same person serve in both capacities, choosing a separate mediator may be preferable.

Chapter 25

MEDIATE OR ARBITRATE?

"An ounce of mediation is worth a pound of
arbitration and a ton of litigation."

JOSEPH GRYNBAUM

Ever wonder whether arbitration might be a better choice than mediation for a client in a particular case? What should you be aware of and think about? Although the purpose of this book is to focus on mediation, some basic information on arbitration may be useful.

Arbitration is a consensual, private, enforceable (unless agreed to as non-binding), non-judicial method of arriving at a decision as to who should win and who should lose and includes the relief or remedies the prevailing party is entitled to. This dispute resolution mechanism has long been employed in the United States. Abraham Lincoln and other lawyers of his era (the 1840s and 1850s) used both binding and non-binding arbitration.

Unlike a mediator, an arbitrator is a decision maker. Like a mediator, the arbitrator is a neutral. Customarily there is either one arbitrator or there are three. When there is one, the parties frequently agree on the person who shall serve, or if they cannot agree, an independent entity will choose one for them. When there are three, it is not uncommon for each party to pick one arbitrator and then allow those two to select the third one. If the parties cannot agree, however, an independent entity will select the arbitrators. The prevailing party is determined by majority vote when three arbitrators are chosen.

As discussed above, although the parties frequently select the arbitrator(s), this is not always the case. They may prefer that an independent entity, such as the American Arbitration Association, select them. Or, in some instances a contract between the parties containing an arbitration clause provides that an independent entity shall select the arbitrator(s).

Arbitration is often employed in the resolution of commercial disputes and is binding more often than not. Non-binding arbitration, however, can provide the parties a mechanism for use in settlement discussions as they seek to avoid a trial. Arbitration may be voluntary but may also be mandatory, as when a contract between the parties contains a clause requiring arbitration whenever a dispute arises.

A contract between the parties containing an arbitration clause may specify that arbitration is mandatory as soon as a dispute occurs. Or, such a contract may require initial good faith negotiations, and if a resolution is not reached within an established time period, mandatory arbitration. Or, it may require mediation followed by mandatory arbitration if the mediation does not result in a settlement, *i.e.*, Med-Arb as discussed in Chapter 24.

Prior to an arbitration, the parties customarily enter into a written Agreement to Arbitrate. That agreement sets out mutually agreed on procedure for conducting the arbitration, including what rules shall be followed and the powers of the arbitrator. An advantage of arbitration versus a trial is flexibility. The parties can incorporate or modify an existing set of rules used by an arbitration provider or create their own.

Discovery commonly occurs before the arbitration hearing. This procedure will include productions and exchanges of documents and the taking of depositions. A pre-arbitration hearing conference, during which the arbitrator and parties discuss the procedure and rules to be followed, is also common. A timetable is established for discovery, motions, briefs, pre-hearing written submissions of evidence, post-hearing briefs and submissions, and the date by which a decision, called an "award," is to be made by the arbitrator(s).

The advantages typically cited for arbitration are:

1. Choice of the decision maker.
2. Efficiency resulting from speedier resolution.
3. Cost savings over a trial.
4. Convenience, because the parties pick the time and place for the hearing and also set the schedule for discovery, briefing, etc.
5. Flexibility in setting up the rules and procedures to be followed, including relaxation of the formal rules of evidence.
6. Confidentiality, because an arbitration hearing is not a public court proceeding.
7. Finality, because the arbitration award is enforceable with only very limited rights of appeal.

The disadvantages typically cited for arbitration are:

1. It is more expensive than mediation because it may require extensive discovery and case preparation, as well as substantial arbitrator(s) fees.
2. A concern is that the arbitrator(s) will "split the baby," that is give each side part of what they wanted, leaving both dissatisfied.
3. Discovery may be more limited than desired by a party.
4. An arbitration award is, for the most part, not appealable.
5. An arbitration award is not directly enforceable. A party seeking to enforce an award against a recalcitrant party must file an action in court to "confirm" the award.

After the hearing and any post-hearing briefs or submissions, the arbitrator(s) renders the "award," the written decision stating who wins and who loses. This decision also sets out any remedies for the prevailing party. Significantly, an arbitrator has the power "to do equity," to make decisions based on what the arbitrator regards as "fairness."

Depending upon what the parties request, the award may either be "reasoned" or "non-reasoned." A reasoned award contains an explanation for the decision made and relief granted, if any. A non-reasoned award simply states who wins and any relief granted without an explanation of the basis for the decision.

Possible remedies which may be granted in an award include:

1. Money damages.
2. Making a declaration as to any matter to be determined.
3. Injunctive relief.
4. Specific performance.
5. Attorneys fees and expenses.
6. Costs of the arbitration including payment of the arbitrator's fees by the losing party.

Variations in arbitration that control the relief which may be granted may be specified. One such variation is "High/Low" or "Bracketed" arbitration which is similar to a "high/low" agreement at a trial. No matter the monetary relief granted or not granted by the arbitrator(s), what will actually be payable is subject to an agreed upon upper and lower limit.

Another variation is "Baseball Arbitration" in which the parties each submit a proposed number and the arbitrator must choose one. The reasoning here is the parties will be more reasonable in their positions for resolution of the dispute.

As stated earlier, grounds for overturning an arbitrator's award are very limited. The common ones include:

1. The award was procured by corruption or fraud.
2. Evident partiality or corruption in the arbitrator(s).
3. Misconduct on the part of the arbitrator(s) in refusing to allow a justified postponement of a hearing, or refusing to hear evidence, or where arbitrator powers are exceeded or imperfectly executed.
4. A manifest disregard of the law, which must be more than an error or misunderstanding with respect to the law. It involves knowing a governing legal principle yet refusing to apply it or ignoring it altogether.

Because of its greater complexity, and a party's lack of control over outcome, many lawyers prefer mediation over arbitration for dispute resolution, but there are still cases for which arbitration may be a wise choice or an actual requirement.

Chapter 26

EARLY NEUTRAL EVALUATION

"A person with a new idea is a crank until the idea succeeds."

MARK TWAIN

Although the focus of this book is mediation, as with the discussion of arbitration in the preceding chapter, some basic information on Early Neutral Evaluation may be useful. This process was pioneered in the 1980s by courts in California. Although it has not yet been used extensively across the United States, it is becoming more widely known and it has the potential to be a valuable tool in resolving cases.

Early Neutral Evaluation is different from arbitration and mediation. It is a hybrid process that, when used successfully, will save time and money for those involved in a legal dispute. Attorneys familiar with the process may even recommend its use before a complaint is filed, however, it would most often be used after a complaint is filed. Its use is best in situations where either the facts are not complex or the facts and the issues are thought to be sufficiently understood by the parties so that extensive discovery is not needed.

There may be some variants in Early Neutral Evaluation procedure depending upon where it is used, by whom and how it has been modified. At its heart, however, it is an informal, non-binding mini-trial by a neutral which is often followed by mediation. Among its benefits are reduced costs, an earlier discussion of a possible settlement opportunity and an actual earlier settlement. Even if a settlement is not immediately achieved, this process can result in a narrowing of issues and the development of a plan for key discovery or other work needed for future negotiations.

Early Neutral Evaluation provides a neutral evaluator's "best professional guess" as to what a judge or jury would do based upon the law and known facts. The neutral evaluator does not decide who is right and who is wrong and has no power to make any binding decisions. Rather, the purpose of the process is to provide a private and confidential opportunity to obtain an opinion about the relative strengths and weaknesses of the parties' evidence and legal positions. The neutral evaluator tries to help the parties predict what the trier of fact may decide. What is sought is an independent second opinion on the merits of a legal dispute. At the same time, however, the neutral evaluator explains only his or her analysis and does not advocate a position or opinion.

The process for an Early Neutral Evaluation is informal. It is also confidential because it is considered to be part of settlement negotiations. Typically a preliminary conference of the neutral and counsel, or other representative for a party such as a claims adjuster, is held to discuss and agree on procedure and rules the parties would like followed. Issues to be addressed will be identified. Use of stipulations, affidavits and live witness presentations (as opposed to formal testimony) will be discussed. Areas that need to be evaluated will be identified to include: (1) claims; (2) defenses; (3) significance of established law; (4) likely verdict; (5) range of damages if the plaintiff prevails; and, (6) settlement value.

In the initial conference, the schedule for the evaluation session will also be established, as will the date for submission of written position papers discussing the facts and law being relied upon. The submissions will be provided sufficiently before the session so that the evaluator will have time to adequately review them. They will also be provided to the opposing party. As is the process, the position papers are confidential as part of settlement discussions and may not be used for any other purpose. They are to be provided to no one other than the neutral, clients, client representatives, and opposing counsel. They will not be provided to a judge nor be admissible in any legal proceeding.

Unlike as in mediation, however, substantive oral ex parte communications with the neutral evaluator prior to the evaluation session are prohibited. The only pre-session substantive communication will be the party's position paper.

The evaluation session is confidential and not recorded. The evaluator makes opening remarks on the process and procedure to be followed, and the parties then make their presentations and responsive presentations. The evaluator may ask questions on the facts or law and seek to clarify areas in dispute that he or she will evaluate for the parties. At the close of the session, the evaluator takes the prior submissions and presentations under consideration. The evaluator may also invite post-session submissions to be provided in a timely manner.

After review of the parties' submissions, and consideration of their presentations, the evaluator privately prepares a written evaluation of the areas to be addressed. In it, the evaluator explains the basis for the opinions reached.

Following completion of the written evaluation, the parties are given the option of jointly hearing the evaluation or, first, of engaging in settlement discussions with the evaluator assisting in the negotiations. If the parties desire that the evaluator assist in settlement discussions, private caucus sessions with the evaluator will follow, just as in mediation. If the parties want to hear the evaluator's opinions and conclusions before doing anything further, they are provided; afterwards the parties may ask for the assistance of the evaluator in settlement discussions or choose not to discuss settlement at all.

The parties have five options following the evaluation session. They are:

(1) Hear the evaluation and do nothing further at that point.
(2) Hear the evaluation and move into settlement discussions.
(3) Postpone hearing the evaluation and move into settlement discussions.
(4) Postpone hearing the evaluation and agree upon a plan for further development of certain areas necessary for possible future settlement discussions and/or trial.
(5) Hear the evaluation and agree upon a plan for further development of certain areas necessary for possible future settlement discussions and/or trial.

In summary, the neutral evaluator's role is to:

* Provide a forum for the parties to set out their positions.
* Analyze the issues presented.
* Assess the evidence and law relied upon by each party.
* Encourage the parties to consider settlement.
* Assist in settlement discussions when requested.
* If the case does not settle, assist the parties in developing a plan for what needs to be accomplished before settlement discussions or a trial occur.

Obviously, Early Neutral Evaluation is not appropriate for all cases. For some, however, this option can save the parties a great deal of time and expense. This process has been used in personal injury, medical malpractice, construction and general civil litigation matters. In locations where it has been used, the lawyers involved stated they liked the process. Typical positive comments from attorneys include the following: there is an early face-to-face setting out of positions; a client concerned about cost or the time involved in litigation will appreciate the process; and, clients who "want their day in court" are provided the opportunity to have their case heard by someone who, although a neutral and unable to issue a legally binding decision, is an authority figure who will satisfy that need.

Early Neutral Evaluation is a process that appears to be on its way to more widespread use.

Chapter 27

SPECIAL MASTERS AND MEDIATION

*"The parties have enough stress between their clients
and the court so I [as special master] try to be viewed
as a safe haven for the discussion of legal issues."*

REEVES NEAL

Why a brief discussion of special masters? Because they sometimes are asked by the parties to assist in settlement discussions by mediating their case.

Both federal and state courts use special masters. The role of the special master is to assist a court in some specific aspect(s) of a case determined by the judge. This role may be limited or broad depending on the complexity of the case and the needs of the court and/or the parties. The court delegates certain authority to the special master; however, a special master is only a tool used by a court and does not supplant the judge's role.

Special masters are helpful when judges' dockets are crowded and do not allow the time necessary to resolve questions or issues in a complex matter as promptly as all, including the judge, would like. They help reduce delays that would otherwise result in increased costs and attorney and client frustrations.

A full discussion of the role of special masters, and the many duties they may perform, is not the purpose of this chapter. It simply is to discuss a special master's potential role in getting a case settled.

I have served as a special master involving a variety of duties in a number of cases in state and federal courts. In most cases I was ultimately asked by the parties to mediate or assist in settlement discussions, and most of these were resolved before it was necessary to submit a special master's report to the court.

A special master learns a great deal about a case, thus enabling him to be very direct with the parties. When the special master assists in settlement discussions prior to filing a report, the parties may sense which way the wind is blowing. This "reality check" can be useful to the lawyers in private settlement discussions which follow.

Lawyers sometimes express concerns about the expense of a special master's fee. However, after the opportunity to work with one, particularly when the special master is able to assist in resolving the case, many have concluded that the use of a special master has saved their clients time and money.

Chapter 28

KEYS TO SUCCESS/KEYS TO FAILURE

"Success is where preparation and opportunity meet."

BOBBY UNSER

"Failure – when most of our so called reasoning consists in finding arguments for going on believing as we already do."

JAMES HARVEY ROBINSON

U sing the definitions of success in Chapter 1, "the accomplishment of an aim or purpose" and "the favorable outcome of something attempted," here are the keys that I believe lead to success or lead to failure.

KEYS TO SUCCESS

* Remembering what "success" is.
* Not being afraid to mediate - what have you got to lose?

* Picking the right time to mediate.
* Picking the right mediator.
* When court-ordered, not assuming a negative attitude.
* Preparing:
    Yourself;
    Your client;
    Your mediator;
    Your opponent.
* Having a "make peace," not a "make war," mindset.
* Using "make peace," not "make war," advocacy – it's not a jury trial.
* Remembering that a purpose of your advocacy is to create doubt in the mind of opponents; most often it will be unlikely you persuade them that you are right.
* Maintaining flexibility.
* Knowing about psychological barriers that get in the way, particularly advocacy and certainty biases.
* Understanding what mediators do and why – they want to help you and your client make realistic assessments and decisions.
* Moving from "advocate" to "counselor" at the appropriate time.
* Exercising patience, even when it is very difficult because of the slow pace of a mediation.
* Keeping your mediator involved in follow-up negotiations when the case doesn't settle at the mediation; don't give up.

KEYS TO FAILURE

* Thinking that "succeeding" and "winning" are the same thing – succeeding is getting a result for a client that makes sense because of the risks and uncertainties of a trial.
* Mediating too soon.
* Using the wrong mediator.

* Failing to prepare:
    Yourself;
    Your client;
    Your mediator;
    Your opponent.
* Holding on to a "make war," not "make peace" mindset.
* Using "make war," not "make peace" advocacy.
* Being inflexible.
* Not being aware of psychological barriers, particularly advocacy and certainty biases.
* Making a substantial change in a pre-mediation demand or offer without sufficient advance notice.
* Surprising the other side with new information.
* Starting with unreasonable demands or offers.
* Overreacting to initial demands or offers.
* Being impatient.
* Walking out when your mediator believes you should stay.
* Giving up and not keeping your mediator involved if the case doesn't settle.

As you keep the above keys to success and keys to failure in mind, I hope they help you represent your clients in mediations and in achieving a successful result, an ending that both they, and you, believe makes sense and is in their best interests.

APPENDIX A

A MEDIATION CHECKLIST

* Know and remember what "success" is. (Chapter 1)
* Think about what mediation is and isn't. (Chapter 2)
* Pick the right time to mediate. (Chapter 6)
* Pick the right mediator. (Chapter 8)
* Prepare yourself. (Chapter 10)
* Prepare your client. (Chapter 11)
* Prepare your mediator. (Chapter 12)
* Prepare your opponent. (Chapter 13)
* Enter with a "make peace" mindset. (Chapter 14)
* Use "make peace" advocacy. (Chapter 14)
* Keep an open mind and be flexible during negotiations. (Chapter 15)
* For a multi-party case, think about the special challenges presented. (Chapter 16)
* For a business dispute, think about how to advise clients and possible creative solutions. (Chapter 17)

* Think about psychological reactions that frequently occur and create barriers that must be overcome for settlement. (Chapter 18)
* Think about what mediators may do to assist in reaching a settlement. (Chapter 19)
* Think about some of the "Don'ts:" (Chapter 21)

> Don't change a pre-mediation demand/offer;
>
> Don't start with an unreasonable demand/offer;
>
> Don't surprise your opponent with new information;
>
> Don't use trial advocacy instead of "make peace" advocacy;
>
> Don't overreact to an initial demand/offer;
>
> Don't be impatient;
>
> Don't walk out when your mediator asks you to stay;
>
> Don't fail to shift from advocate to counselor when needed to get a settlement that makes sense for your client; and
>
> Don't give up. Keep your mediator involved in post-mediation discussions when the case does not settle.

APPENDIX B

AN ADR PROGRAM'S RECOMMENDATIONS
FOR A SUCCESSFUL MEDIATION

REMEMBER: Virtually all civil cases settle prior to trial. Come to the mediation prepared to settle rather than waiting to do so the day before, or the morning of, the trial.

REMEMBER: Surprises at mediation on liability or damages significantly reduce the likelihood of success.

PLAINTIFF(S): Provide all information on damages claimed in advance of the mediation. Insurance carriers customarily review claims, and decide on a range of what they are willing to pay, based upon information available prior to the day of the mediation. When an insurance carrier is not involved, defendants will have come to a position based upon what they know about a case. The more substantial the case, the farther in advance of the mediation date such information needs to be supplied.

DEFENDANT(S): At the time a mediation date is selected, ask counsel for the plaintiff(s) if there is additional information on damages claimed or liability which plaintiffs' counsel wishes to have considered. Explain that the decision on what the defendant will be willing to pay to settle the case will be based upon information obtained prior to the mediation.

PLAINTIFF(S) AND DEFENDANT(S): Complete sufficient fact and damages discovery prior to the mediation. It is important that the significant facts pertinent to liability and damages are known. (Unfortunately, a mediation may begin and, not long into it, counsel may realize additional deposition testimony or other discovery is necessary before the case can be settled.)

PLAINTIFF(S): Make a pre-mediation demand.

DEFENDANT(S): Make a pre-mediation offer.

PLAINTIFF(S): Don't increase your pre-mediation demand at mediation unless there is truly something significantly new that justifies it. If there is such new information, make it known to counsel for the defendant prior to the mediation.

DEFENDANT(S): Don't decrease your last pre-mediation offer at mediation unless there is truly something significantly new that justifies it. If there is such new information, make it known to counsel for the plaintiff prior to the mediation.

PLAINTIFF(S) AND DEFENDANT(S): Explain the mediation process and discuss the strengths and weaknesses of the case with your client prior to the mediation.

REMEMBER: There is an important difference from a trial in the manner of presentation at mediation. Your purpose should be to discuss the strengths of your case and the weaknesses of the other side's in a calm, rational manner. Confrontational and unnecessarily hostile presentations will make reaching a settlement much more difficult.

REMEMBER: Compromise is required. Neither side is likely to get everything it would like. Focus on what is in your client's best interests in ending the litigation.

LASTLY: Don't be discouraged if the case doesn't settle the day of mediation. Many cases settle after the mediation session because the stage for further settlement discussions has been set. Consider scheduling fol-low-up telephone discussions with your mediator that continue the pre-vious settlement negotiations. Your mediator should want to continue to work with the parties so that a settlement can be reached.

APPENDIX C

_____

_____

<u>AGREEMENT TO MEDIATE</u>

For good consideration by mutual promises, RAYMOND G. CHADWICK, the Mediator, and the undersigned parties and their counsel hereby agree to mediate this legal dispute as follows:

1. MEDIATION PROCESS. Mediation is a non-adversarial settlement negotiation that can only result in a resolution if all parties voluntarily agree. Nothing is mandatory in the mediation process.
2. GOOD FAITH. By signing this agreement, all parties pledge to cooperate and participate in good faith in all mediation sessions and to use their best efforts to obtain a mutual agreement.
3. MEDIATOR'S ROLE. The Mediator, although an attorney, will not act as a judge, nor as an attorney, and will not offer legal or financial advice to any party in the mediation. The Mediator

shall be neutral and only act to facilitate a mutual agreement between the parties. The Mediator's opinions, suggestions, or advice, if any, shall not be binding on anyone. All legal advice will be provided by counsel for each party.

4. CAUCUS. The Mediator may convene a caucus (private meeting) with parties and their counsel, for clarification of issues. Information developed during the caucus may be confidential between such parties and the Mediator, as indicated at the time by the parties or their counsel. Such information will not be shared unless permission of the party or their counsel providing the information is obtained.

5. CONFIDENTIAL AND PRIVILEGED. The undersigned parties agree that this mediation process is confidential in nature. The parties agree that the communications occurring during the course of the mediation, including pre-mediation and post-mediation discussions with the Mediator are confidential. Except to the extent that a Court of competent jurisdiction requires any person or party to this mediation to disclose such information, each person and party to this mediation agrees to maintain the confidentiality of this mediation and agrees not to make public (a) the views or suggestions made by it or another party with respect to possible settlement of the dispute, (b) admissions made by another party in the course of the mediation proceedings, proposals made or views expressed by the mediator, (c) proposals made or views expressed by the Mediator, or (d) the conduct of any party during the course of the mediation.

All parties agree not to institute any action based on the mediation or to subpoena the Mediator to testify or to produce any records at any future legal proceedings. If any party does so, that party hereby agrees to indemnify and hold the Mediator harmless for any liability, expense and cost, including attorney fees, incurred by the Mediator as a result of such action.

6. TERMINATION. The Mediator retains the power to terminate this mediation if at any time the Mediator believes that further discussion is highly unlikely to lead to resolution, that one or

more parties lacks authority or discretion to resolve the case, or that one or more parties is not acting in good faith to resolve the disputes between them. The Mediator will work diligently to persuade the parties to continue discussions during and after the mediation conference if the Mediator believes that resolution or partial resolution is feasible.

7. LIABILITY. The Mediator is acting as a facilitator to assist the parties in various means of resolving their dispute. It is agreed that absent misconduct, fraud or gross negligence, the Mediator shall not be subject to liability to the parties as a result of his service as the Mediator.

8. ADMINISTRATION COST AND MEDIATION FEES. The Mediator is providing mediation services in this matter at a rate of $_____ per party per hour.

READ AND ACCEPTED:

This the _____ day of _____, 20__

Signature:_____ Print Name:_____
                                Title:_____

Signature:_____ Print Name:_____
                                Title:_____

Signature:_____ Print Name:_____
                                Title:_____

Signature:_____ Print Name:_____
                                Title:_____

MEDIATOR:

Signature:_____ Print Name:_____

APPENDIX D

SETTLEMENT AGREEMENT MEMORANDUM

The Plaintiff(s)_____

_____

_____

Has/have agreed to accept, and the Defendant(s)_____

_____

_____

Has/have agreed to pay the sum of $_____

_____

Subject to the following terms:_____

_____

_____

(see attached if necessary).

This _____ day of_____, 20 _____.

PLAINTIFF(S) AND   DEFENDANT(S) AND/OR
ATTORNEYS
ATTORNEY FOR PLAINTIFF(S):   FOR DEFENDANT(S):

_____   _____

_____   _____

_____   _____

This Settlement Agreement Memorandum contains all the essential elements of the terms and conditions of the settlement in this case. This is intended as a written memorandum of a binding Settlement Agreement resolving all claims arising from the above legal dispute. The formal settlement documents will be prepared and executed by all parties as soon as possible.

_____

NEUTRAL'S SIGNATURE

Plaintiff(s)   Defendant(s)

_____   _____

_____   _____

Counsel for Plaintiff(s)   Counsel for Defendant(s)

_____   _____

_____   _____

_____

Mediator

APPENDIX E

MEDIATED SETTLEMENT AGREEMENT
MEMORANDUM OF AGREED TERMS

_____	)	Court:_____
	)	
vs.	)	Case No.:_____
	)	
_____	)	

The above-named parties have settled this Action effective with the execution of this agreement. It sets forth all terms agreed to and the parties recognize and agree that such terms are binding and enforceable.

The terms of the Mediated Settlement Agreement Memorandum are as follows:

_____

_____

_____

_____

_____

_____

_____
_____
_____
_____
_____
_____
_____
_____
_____
_____
_____
_____
_____
_____
_____
_____
_____
_____
_____
_____
_____
_____
_____
_____
_____
_____

The parties hereby obligate themselves to fully cooperate in effectuating the terms of this agreement and to the preparation of any documents necessary to its fulfillment and enforcement.

Not as a condition of settlement, but as an additional obligation of the parties, in the event the parties cannot agree on the final language of any final settlement or other documents to be prepared, the parties agree to mediate such dispute(s).

This _____ day of _____, 20_____.

_____   _____

PLAINTIFF   DEFENDANT

_____   _____

ATTORNEY(S) FOR PLAINTIFF   ATTORNEY(S) FOR DEFENDANT

This Mediated Settlement Agreement Memorandum Agreed to Terms contains settlement terms agreed to, and has been represented to the mediator signing below as a binding settlement pursuant to the mediation conducted by such mediator.

_____

MEDIATOR'S SIGNATURE